To David—

# JOGGING IN HAVANA

(Short Stories)

Best wishes,
Cyril Dabydeen
March 2, 01

# JOGGING IN HAVANA
## (Short Stories)

by

CYRIL DABYDEEN

Mosaic Press
Oakville-New York-London

CANADIAN CATALOGUING IN PUBLICATION DATA

Dabydeen, Cyril 1945-
Jogging in Havana

ISBN 0-88962-525-5 (bound) ISBN 0-88962-526-3 (pbk.)

I. Title.

PR8557.A29J6 1992 C813'.54 C92-094969-X
PR9199.3.D23J6 1992



Published by MOSAIC PRESS, P.O. Box 1032, Oakville, Ontario, L6J 5E9, Canada. Offices and warehouse at 1252 Speers Road, Units #1&2, Oakville, Ontario L6L 5N9, Canada.

Mosaic Press acknowledges the assistance of the Canada Council and the Ontario Arts Council in support of this publishing programme


Design by
Typeset by Jackie Ernst

Printed and bound in Canada

ISBN 0-88962-525-5 HC 0-88962-526-3 PB

MOSAIC PRESS:
In Canada:
MOSAIC PRESS, 1252 Speers Road, Units #1&2, Oakville, Ontario L6L 5N9, Canada. P.O. Box 1032, Oakville, Ontario L6J 5E9
In the United States:
Distributed to the trade in the United States by: National Book Network, Inc., 4720-A Boston Way, Lanham, MD, 20705, U.S.A.
In the U.K.
John Calder (Publishers) Ltd., 9-15 Neal Street, London, WCZH 9TU, England.

## ACKNOWLEDGEMENTS

Some of these stories first appeared in an original form in the following magazines and anthologies:

"A Plan in a Plan," *The Dalhousie Review* (Winter 1982-83);

"The Rink," *The Fiddlehead,* (Spring 1985);

"The Puja-Man," *The Toronto South Asian Review* (Summer 1986);

"Places," *New Canadian Review* (Winter 1990-91);

"Jogging in Havana," *The Canadian Fiction Magazine* (#70, 1990);

"All the King's Men," *The University of Windsor Review* (1992); and

"God Save the Queen," *The New Quarterly* (Winter 92/93).

"A Plan is a Plan" also appeared in *Other Voices: Writings by Blacks in Canada* (Williams-Wallace Publishers, 1985).

"The Rink," also appeared in *Language at Work* (Holt, Rinehart and Winston, 1987); and in *Breaking Through: A Canadian Literary Mosaic* (Prentice-Hall, 1989).

"Ain't Got no Cash" appeared in *A Shapely Fire: Changing the Literary Landscape* (Mosaic Press, 1987).

## TABLE OF CONTENTS

# ONE

# PLACES

They used to say to me, "Open your eyes on him." But Anil, my brother's son, wouldn't be deterred. He'd crawl in and out of the house, with no one seeming to know what he was up to. And, indeed, my brother and his wife were unable to "control" him. Sighing, they surmised that Anil had wickedness in him from the day he was born.

My brother shook his head. His wife Delia repeated what he said: and somehow this seemed to be based on fate, the way life was meant to be. It was the same fate that governed life in the entire village, though now my brother and his wife had moved from the village to the town. I figured they wondered if it was this that really caused the change in Anil.

Anil's unpredictabililty confused, troubled, them in a way. And then the government was also blamed. Nothing in the country was going well; everyone seemed unhappy, an overall bitterness in the air. Some blamed it squarely on socialism, a new form of government; and once in a while in the discussion about socialism, Cuba or Moscow would be mentioned, though not often. Beneath it all, people were really frightened.

Not Anil!

I was home then. And I knew a lot was expected of him: he, their first child. All the villagers expected their children to do well at school; they'd tell the young ones about their relatives abroad, the role models. In our case, they'd tell Anil about me. And in the letters too, I knew this (though the letters weren't too regular); and I often guessed what the replies would be: going to live in the town caused a dramatic change in their lives.

"Uncle...he coming! You be careful now, Anil. You must have good manners," they said to Anil.

But he jeered, laughed. It was Anil's way.

Delia, my brother's wife, became exasperated. A really shy girl when I first knew her, almost dour: she was also stubbborn, really "opening" her eyes on Anil from time to time. And now, because I was coming home once again (such was the talk, rumour), stubbornness prevailed more than ever. Some members of the family would say that Delia's stubbornness had passed on to Anil. Just look at him, you'd see it. My brother repeated this, and laughed.

Delia scowled heavily.

When my brother laughed again, it seemed he was mocking her.

Anil, as if inspired by the laughter, ran across the neighbour's yard and mounted the tall *jamoon* tree. He stood on the flimsiest branch, like a large bird or monkey, flaunting–and yelling to everyone to watch him, to see how good he was.

"Look–see, everyone...Yes, see!" he yelled again, hanging with one hand, his right leg lifted in the air, his dark eyes bright, his hair scattered about his face as a strong wind blew. The tree shook, bent almost.

Anil laughed, twisting, leaning forward, wanting to let go with both hands...Oh, God. Anil was now a trapeze artist–some of the neighbours, laughing, said: these same townspeople, mostly Africans, who weren't always used to our East Indian ways. Yes, Anil might one day leave the country and go to places like Brazil where he'd become a real trapeze artist! Laughter, real guffaws. They kept looking at Anil all the while.

The tree shook again.

Anil once more let go both his hands, pretending he was about to fall.

Delia dashed across the yard ready to flail, to bawl out–as the townspeople watched how the East Indians behaved. Very agitated, Delia shouted: "Boy, come down at once! Come down, before you fall an' break yuh ass!"

Anil jeered even more, defying her; defying everyone in a way.

A stronger wind blew, the entire branch, tree, shaking. A wider smile on Anil's face: he seemed younger than his nine years.

The crowd grew larger, awe on their faces; others, though, kept on laughing, while some were still anxious. They watched Anil, waiting to see when he'd fall...when his body would be splattered on the ground about thirty yards below.

But Anil was bent on putting on a real show.

Delia was about to swoon with anxiety. "Boy, come down! Come down at once, before you fall an' break yuh ass–you hear me!"

Anil still ignored her; then he saw his little sister, Sarah, tugging at her mother's hip; only four–she was. Anil waved to her, his face brightening with a large smile.

She waved back, smiling, then laughing.

"Sarah, Sarah," he sang, hands still in the air like a tight-rope walker.

"Oh God," let out Delia. "Wait until yuh fader come, eh. He go break yuh ass wid lashes!"

The townspeople tittered. And Anil, as if only for them–to show them he could defy anyone–flaunted even more.

Sarah tugged, tightened her hold on her mother's skirt, her hands tense. And it seemed that the townspeople secretly loved this show, it was a comedy provided by the East Indians; a few, however, were intrigued as they watched Delia's face, her fear.

An hour later Anil slowly came down the tree, when the crowd had almost dispersed. By then Delia was exhausted with worry; it was no use scolding anymore. One older man said: "That Anil, he has the devil in he."

Delia immediately eyed him, stubbornness revving up in her. No one dared speak evil of her son. From a distance and now holding Sarah's hand, Anil merely laughed, his teeth glinting in the sunlight.

When his father came home and heard what he'd done, he took out his belt and started wallopping Anil. After the first few blows–as expected–Anil screamed, "Murder! Murder!"

His father sprinted after him, late though in the afternoon as it was–racing after Anil across the wide cemetery along the Stanleytown main road.

Delia straggled behind, Sarah still with her. "Ow, man, don't kill he," she said. "He just mannish, dat's all."

The townspeople watched from their windows, some–the women–laughing.

Delia's voice rose: "Ow, man, don't kill he. He just mannish!"

The others lipped the words, like a refrain. A heavy wind was blowing against their faces; they seemed really happy.

Not Delia; she was almost sick with worry.

My brother, sprinting after Anil, hopped over gravetsones–the two of them like rabbits. Anil fell, but quickly got up–and sprinted forward again.

It was now almost dark; and they were like two racing apparitions. Delia was still somewhere far behind.

My brother was now exhausted.

Anil, sensing this, stopped running; he circled and bent low behind a gravestone. Then when his father wasn't looking, he hopped over the next gravestone; he seemed to have disappeared, thought his father, sighing and slowly walking home.

Anil followed behind, closer.

His father didn't turn back, spent as he was. In a way though,he was glad Anil feared him–really fearing a good wallop. He didn't want him to be misbehaved. In his mind he was telling him to emulate me--the one abroad.

Anil waited outside the house until it was late that night, the chase over the gravestones fresh on his mind. On his father's mind as well. It was a cat-and-mouse game now. Delia, from time to time, looked out the window–to see if Anil was still there, still biding his time when to come in.

Her husband was dour. He growled something or the other.

Twenty minutes later Delia looked out the window again. She called out to Anil, "Come in, now; he won't kill you!"

Anil remained steadfast outside. Glum. He dug his toes in the soft mud, the night blacker, the neighbours now in bed; though one or two listened to the quiet drama enacted, and from time to time they got up and peeped through the jalousie–to see if Anil was still outside, like a sentinel.

Delia–again–"Come in, now, before yuh fader really get mad."

Anil dug his toes deeper in the ground, aware of the neighobours peeping at him; he wanted sympathy from them in a way. One or two of them said: "Go in, now, boy; don't give your fader more badderation. Go in before he kill yuh. Go...when your mother calls." This was said out of a sense of good neighbourliness

Anil, as if heeding this advice, took a few steps towards the door, inching forward.

Delia was aware of what Anil was up to, biding his time. She looked at her husband, how dour he still was.

Anil was at the door.

Delia, a little circumspect at first, then quickly–with lightning speed almost and completely taking Anil by surprise–opened the door and pulled him.

As if he was the injured one, Anil began to cry. This was his defence, playing on their sympathy; he was their first child after all. They loved him, didn't they?

His father, eating his supper,was grim-faced. He showed his anger by not saying anything; though he was aware of Anil's every move.

Delia scolded, "You must obey yuh fader, Anil." Her tone was conciliatory now, Anil's tears having this effect on her. And in a way she was glad Anil was no longer outside for the neighbours to snicker.

Anil remained standing in a corner, head lowered, contrite.

Delia added, "You shouldn't be climbing dat tree! What if yuh fall an' break yuh ass?"

Anil kept his head lowered; he watched his father eating.

Delia added, "An' running over the graveyard...what for, eh? Only dead people does be in graveyard. Boy, you not fraid or what?"

Anil lifted his head manfully. He declared: "Dead people doan frighten me." His voice was firm, as if he was suddenly in control.

His father stopped eating. He eyed Anil sideways.

Anil stared at his father, even more manfully.

In a heavy tone his father said, "So you not afraid of dead people, eh?"

Anil shook his head.

Delia at once asked, "What yuh fraid of then?"

"Nothing."

"Nothing, eh?" His father once more asked.

Anil's eyes shifted to his father's belt close by on the table, the same one that his father carried with him when he'd chased after him across the gravestones. Then he looked at the door; it was within reach; he could make a dash for it, if necessary.

"Boy, you not fraid–not even of yuh fader?" Delia's tone was consistently reprimmanding.

Anil looked looked at the belt on the table again. He didn't reply.

Delia continued, "Boy, you hear what I say?"

Anil slowly nodded; but this was too half-hearted for Delia. And she was really pressing for a full answer, for her husband's satisfaction.

"So?" she added, waiting to hear more from him.

When Anil didn't answer, she reddened. "Boy, you prappa mannish or what? Spit an' lick it up!"

This was the worst punishment, an unbearable humiliation; and Anil stood his ground, eyeing the door once more.

His father noted Anil glancing at the door, and he searched with his eyes for the belt: to see if it was within reach.

Delia again said, "Boy, you hear what I say?"

Anil didn't even nod this time, as she expected him to do. Inwardly she began fretting, because a crisis was once more developing. Anil remained still as stone.

Delia, more impatient now, said, "Boy, you deaf or what?"

Anil moved a few inches backward, his thoughts on the door. His father began getting up slowly.

Anil moved a couple of inches towards the door, his muscles tense.

Delia also became tense. She cast a sideways glance at her husband, noting his dour mood; grim he was.

But his father was also imagining the graveyard, and how tired he was; he didn't look forward to another futile chase. Delia recognized this in her husband and sighed, and shifted attention once again to Anil. In resignation almost, she muttered, "Okay, promise you won't climb dat tree again!"

Silence.

"Promise, you hear me!" Delia raised her voice to a rasp. Anil, sighing hard, murmured, "I...promise."

* * *

Anil had changed a lot, they wrote saying. I was curious to see how much he'd really changed. But it seemed to me, far away in Canada, that Anil would never change. I imagined him from time to time still wilfull, Delia's stubbornness yet in him. Maybe he kept climbing trees, running across the graveyard; and his father had totally given up on him, allowing him to do as he liked. I also imagined Anil mixing well with the townspeople, with a whole bunch of new friends, taller, more confident, holding his own everywhere. Even Delia had given up on him in a way. Once I even dreamt Anil standing on a gravestone late at night, hands akimbo, looking back at his father, and laughing hard.

Weeks, months went by, and I didn't hear from them. Maybe they were still expecting me to come home for a visit. And I was promising myself to do this once more. A letter came in reply to my last. Yes, Anil whom I'd been asking about–had changed. He was really well-behaved.

I smiled. This couldn't be true.

Now he was about eleven or twelve, I couldn't remember which. Anil was nothing like when I'd last seen him, my brother wrote. I sensed Delia behind the writing hand, reassuring me, urging my brother to write only what was good about Anil. Was Anil really standing back with hands akimbo and laughing...at them?

Now I wondered if Anil would remember me.

But in a way it was I who wouldn't recognize him when, finally, I set eyes on him as I'd made the trip home.

Anil was extremely quiet, assessing me; I wasn't sure he remembered me. The animation in him was completely gone.

"How are you, Anil?" I asked, handing him the Canadian T-shirt with "OTTAWA" written in large letters in front.

He barely nodded, taking it, and looked down, eyes dull. Something had happened.

I glanced at Delia. Then at my brother, Anand. They both smiled, pleased with Anil's docility in a way.

Nothing in their manner helped me to understand why he'd changed.

"D'you remember me, Anil?" I asked, putting my arm across his shoulder. He smiled. "No," he replied.

I was hoping he might say yes.

"He's your uncle–the one we been talking bout all along," scolded Delia, raising her voice. "How come you don't remember he, eh?"

And his father added, to me: " He remembers you alright. He jus' playing de fool."

"Come on, Anil, tell," I urged. "Do you remember me?"

I expected a positive answer.

Anil kept his head lowered; and from his eyes–I figured he'd really changed. He was a different Anil now. I looked at Delia, then at my brother.

My brother sensed what was going through my mind, and muttered, "He behaves well."

Delia had a pleased look on her face, as she murmured, "He does everything you ask he to do. He runs errands..." It was as if this change in Anil was really for my benefit.

Was it?

Anil's head was still lowered. I expected, wanted, to see a flash of protest in him.

Nothing.

His sister Sarah, nearby, giggled; she'd grown considerably over the last three years, and she was the one who seemed lively, who was stealing the show from Anil.

My attention on Anil once more, I asked, "Are you still climbing trees?" I laughed a little.

His father also laughed. "Ah, you remember that, eh?"

Sarah giggled again.

Anil lifted his head, and his eyes–they seemed to flash that instant.

I looked at Delia at once, at her own eyes, how they widened too; as if she was reprimmanding him.

"He doesn't do dat anymore," she said. "He's a good boy now." Her eyes truly brightened with pride.

Nothing else was said for a while.

Later Delia, my brother and I talked politics, about the changes taking place in the country, how people were leaving more than ever and going to Canada, New York. Even some of the townspeople were leaving. The corruption (some said) created a real sickness in everyone.

It wasn't just a question of power and race anymore. They asked about Canada. Was it the same? My brother talked about America.

Delia, a little playfully, said, "Maybe when you go back, you can tek Anil wid you." She smiled like a young girl.

I thought she was serious. Her eyes, dark pools.

My brother remained quiet, then he added, " Here it's terrible, you see. He has no future."

Delia added, "Anil's jus' like de Canadians, you know. He behaves well." She looked pointedly at me. Sarah hugged her mother's waist, and giggled.

I looked around for Anil. I hadn't seen him leave.

Delia muttered, "What's it really like in Canada, eh? Change there too, no?" She seemed sceptical, and she gave out a short nervous laugh.

My brother looked at me.

I was still thinking about Anil.

They seemed bored by my response.

My brother, a little irritably now, said, "Here, it's no good. The system of government you know; everyone will leave one day. In Guyana, there's no future."

I felt a little guilty. I figured that they were really thinking about Anil's future. Both of them looked closely at me.

"Life is useless here," Delia affirmed, glancing at her husband.

Sarah hugged her more closely. Delia put a hand on her head, patting it.

Then she too started looking around for Anil.

I was touched by the worry on their faces. Then I thought of the countryside where we'd all grown up, and my brother and I as children: how we'd swim daily in the darkwatered creek close to our village; the fun we had; our house built on stilts, and when it rained heavily–how it flooded almost; how too, we regularly swam in the sugarcane-reeking canals and kept our mouths open when it rained, catching the fat drops and pretending they were pearls! Memory wafting me to another world. Here...now, it was desolation.

I looked once more for Anil.

I spottted him in a corner, listening to us all along, a little surreptitiously. His head was lowered.

I walked up to him, as his parents watched me.

Once more I put an arm on his shoulder. He was really unlike the Anil I knew before. I recalled him whitely clad sprinting over gravestones on a dark night.

Then I asked, "What is it, Anil?"

He shook his head, he didn't want to talk. Not knowing what else to say, I asked:

"Are you doing well at school?"

Delia overheard me, and intervened, "He's de brightest; that's what his teacher say. He always getting high marks." She let out a cackle of a laugh.

I looked at her, the shape of her mouth, her eyes narrowing. Then I looked at my brother: he was looking at Anil. Both parents were saying, Take him to Canada when you return. It seemed they were eager to get rid of him.

I turned to Anil again, studying his manner, his bent head, shyness.

I asked, "D'you want to go back with me to Canada?"

He kept his head lowered.

Delia was eager for him to speak up. Now was his chance, she was saying.

But all Anil did was smile.

Delia was disappointed; and she walked off with Sarah in a huff it seemed.

My brother followed them. And Anil and I were...alone. Maybe they wanted it like this; planned it all along.

My hand still on Anil's shoulder.

"No," he replied to my question about going to Canada, a veiled defiance in him. He looked directly at me.

"Why not?"

He shrugged.

"You want to remain here to climb trees, eh?" I said, laughing, affectionately rubbing his head.

He didn't answer, but right then he looked at me with the customary sparkle in his eyes.

He began talking quickly, excitedly, telling me about all his friends, a whole set of new ones he'd made; how he liked playing with them, for hours sometimes. He'd walk with them to school, walk with them home; he was just like one of them, all Africans. It was so different from my own growing up in the village where nearly everyone was East Indian. (Then, tension between Africans and Indians was only starting to develop all across Guyana, and many of us blamed the politicians for this.)

I hoped the sparkle would remain in Anil's eyes; I also wanted him then to talk about his mother and father. But it was only his friends whom he talked about. He even boasted about them.

I merely muttered, "Ah, your friends, eh?"

He nodded, talking animatedly now.

But it was as if Anil also understood what was going through my mind. He uttered, " They are...*my friends*," and the way he looked at me, he defied me to say otherwise, his eyes sparkling fully.

Thinking back, I realized it was the only serious conversation I had with him.

A few days before my return to Canada, his father said, "That Anil, he has me worried sometimes you know."

"Why?" I asked.

"Something is not right about him. He's too quiet, if you know what I mean."

I didn't, but I quickly added, "He seems well-behaved."

"Oh, I know," mused my brother. "He's well-behaved alright. But there's something else. It just happened overnight. It's like he's a new boy." A worried look was in his eyes.

"A new boy?" I asked, wanting to smile.

"Yes." He was very serious. "You know, we been telling him all along about you in Canada. And sometimes how it's cold there." He looked away, then added, "How cold is it really? How different from here, eh?"

Without waiting for an answer, he continued on: "We're always telling him about you. Maybe Anil might want to go back with you; to stay with you. But now..." he stopped, breathing in hard.

I kept looking at him, how worried he suddenly seemed.

He continued, "We always tell him he had to be well-behaved if you was going to take him with you. Maybe that had an effect on him. What you think, eh?"

He looked forcefully at me, demanding an answer. As if I was the one responsible for the transformation in Anil's personality.

I dwelled on this. Maybe it was thinking about Canada that had this effect on him; not just me.

Then, close to the window as we were, I looked out. Anil was outside playing with his friends.

Suddenly he seemed his usual self, the old Anil I knew, laughing hard, racing up and down, chasing after his friends, they after him, the truly mixed group that they were. Next they seemed all about him, romping, laughing, egging him on; and Anil was chaffing them too, hilarious as he seemed, his face animated; so highspirited he was. They all were; all one.

My brother was also looking out the window.

Anil glanced up at us just then, and he seemed about to wave. Then he stopped.

Delia was close to us at the window now; and maybe this was what made him decide not to wave. He'd suddenly become less animated.

Delia said to me,"I am glad the way he turn out. Now and again though, he still mannish."

She looked at me, wanting my approval. She added, "You won't take he wid you to Canada, eh?"

She said this almost inaudibly, as if she didn't want her husband to hear her. Maybe she merely asked this, as a kind of courtesy, since Anil was my brother's child–and it was expected that they give him up to me; if only as an empty gesture; and I was never meant to take the offer seriously. In a few days we'd be far apart once again, thousands of miles away from each other...and I'd once more be thinking about my brother chasing after his son over gravestones, the old memory dying hard.

And maybe I'd see Anil far ahead of his father, hands akimbo, and all his friends not too far away, rooting for Anil.

My brother asked–quietly–as if he was taking a cue from Delia:

"Maybe one day he will go to Canada or America, also."

I didn't answer. I didn't want to think of Anil in North America. Only here.

But his parents were defying me, the silence heavier; as we kept looking outside.

Suddenly the voices of the others rose, throbbed. A cry rose, goading me to look further out. To look at them. At Anil.

*Say something*!

Or, maybe–say nothing at all.

My mouth clamped shut; and it was my brother's head that lowered slightly this time. Not Anil's. More sounds outside, the boys' exultation; the frenzy of the new place, the town. A new joy, I sensed, defying everyone: the politicians and their systems...and their altogether welcoming a new day...a new country!

# RELATIONS

A distinct, seemingly inevitable, roundness was overtaking Goldie: which happened just about the time her husband started travelling, everyone said. Vernon (he was called Verne) was the silent, taciturn type; smallish, stringy, but strong. He smiled little, and kept to himself most of the time. He was very much unlike Goldie, who laughed with everyone, and even giggled by herself.

The villagers, however,seemed preoccupied with Verne; they constantly kept guessing where he'd go next: if, to the Caribbean islands. No, this time they figured he'd go some place really far, where no one in the country had ever travelled to. And, oddly, they fantasized going to such a place themselves: being in a plane, the sheer thrill and excitement of it; or being in a large ship, which boggled their minds. Then they looked at Goldie, at how bigger she seemed overnight–and laughed.

Goldie also laughed.

It was now rumoured that Verne was involved in shady politics, and Goldie giggled next. Of course, everyone knew Verne was absolutely devoted to the Party; his travelling somehow was tied to this. Once more they looked at Goldie. When she giggled again, she seemed the repository of all that they longed for because they figured that Verne, silent as he was, told her everything about his travels. And Goldie continued getting fatter before their eyes; there was no thought of a word like "elephantiasis," or that her fatness was due to her diet (mainly rice, sometimes mounds of it).

Again they looked at Goldie, with awe. She batted an eyelid, accepting *them*; as much as she accepted Verne–*the traveller*. When Verne came home once more, he looked unlike his usual self, talkative now; then, he reverted to his quiet. Some said quickly that it was his Party work which made him like this. They no longer tried deciphering his thoughts; and for a while no one looked at Goldie. Only I did, as I tried to figure out when Verne would take off again. He did–before I could fully work it out in my mind.

Again, speculation about various countries where he'd gone to: in the Middle East, Far East; Muslim and Christian countries; then Hindu ones (one mentioned India loudly because that was where most of our forebears came from). But another quickly said Africa–he'd gone there, since Africans and their ancestry of slavery were familiar to us. Countries see-sawed in everyone's mind. Only a few thought of the Communist countries. They looked at Goldie: she knew, giggly as she was.

Goldie merely turned to me, her nephew; we'd become closer as the years rolled on. I watched her eyelids drooping, lips bunching forth. And yet she smiled.

Verne stayed away longer than usual this time, almost six months. When he finally came home again, he brought gifts, an assortment of things, all suited to the temperate climate–not the tropics. To Goldie, weather didn't matter. She played at putting on the thick woollen sweater. She immediately looked...gargantuan!

Loud laughter–the neighbours, the nieces, nephews, surrounding her, looking at her, all laughing.

Goldie, as expected, also laughed.

Then she tried taking off the sweater, as it fastened on her shoulder and head. She sweltered, wheezed, and breathed harder.

This time Verne also laughed. And maybe he didn't think Goldie had gotten fatter.

I knew everyone would talk about this for days, Goldie struggling to get the thick, woollen sweater over her head. Maybe Goldie was merely putting on act for everyone, particularly Verne. Even her getting fat was also an act. I didn't know why I kept thinking this.

Verne seemed tired now; he grimaced from time to time, restless, maybe itching to go off again. And, oddly, I began thinking about our country, where we were going, how little the changes taking place were affecting our lives; as if our village was cut off from everywhere else. And it seemed Verne suspected the thoughts going through my mind, because he'd look at me and nod. Then he didn't; maybe he saw things differently. With Verne you never really knew: he who never liked being here too long. I didn't ask him what his true thoughts were. Now, as before, only Goldie held our attention. She fiddled with the Polaroid camera Verne had also brought, playing at taking out pictures of everyone, all gleeful faces around; then, she took one of Verne, holding the camera steady, a wide smile on her face; and fatter than ever she seemed.

Verne grimaced hard, as if suddenly intimidated, discomfitted. Dead serious he was.

I watched them and shook my head, and smiled.

* * *

Verne would one day leave Goldie, he'd never return: this thought came to me quietly, though I must have been thinking about it for a long time. Yes, he'd leave their three children also, all boys, each of whom was well on his way to becoming a rascal; all Goldie's fault–as Verne often reminded her when he came home.

Other people began saying this also, blaming Goldie for this or that, all because she wasn't able to keep Verne at home, when the other husbands, fathers, were at home. Sometimes, mixed feelings prevailed, because there was always the Party, which required travelling...and again they wished they could be like Verne.

Goldie held up the Polaroid camera once more, aiming at the next neighbour who visited (they came as they liked: though not when Verne was at home). Her lips, the lower one especially, kept me glued to her. I recalled how as a young girl, a child really, she always curled in the lip and made a loud sucking sound. *Clack-clack,* like water forced out in a spurt from a small-mouthed jar.

"Stop dat," her mother, my aunt, would bawl at her.

Goldie immediately stopped.

But once her mother looked away, Goldie was at it again; like a reflex action. Maybe it was a sickness–"sucking her lip" all the time.

I watched her steadily, older as I was by two years. Goldie looked at me, and smiled: and again curled her lip; as if just for me–to watch her.

Goldie's mother yearned for her to stop this habit. She wanted Goldie to grow up beautiful, as she said, fair as Goldie was (perhaps fairer than anyone else in the village). I knew she wanted Goldie to look like an Indian movie star, Vijayantimala or Nargis. We'd watch Indian movies at the local cinema, the only recreation people had, the sugar cane workers; and for days after, everyone talked about the episodes, as if they were everyday occurrences in the village. And the stars became household names, and the songs they sang were daily piped to the villages during the "Indian Hour" on the local radio. And they dwelled again and again on how beautiful and handsome the stars were, fantasizing about places like Bombay and Delhi, so far away from Guyana; yet close. And Auntie also watched these movies, with Goldie in her mind—a child star. But by sucking her lip Goldie was thwarting her chances in life.

Auntie and Uncle talked about this from time to time, sometimes arguing. Uncle, though, was really lethargic: he slept most of the day since he worked at nights; he really saw little of Goldie. Auntie did most of the talking, as was to be expected.

When Goldie once more sucked her lip, Auntie threatened, "If you na stop dat, I go put hot pepper on yuh mouth!"

Goldie started crying.

Auntie, soft-hearted, relented.

"Ow, I was only jokin'. Me chile, how I go do dat to you,eh?" Auntie, sentimental, laughed a little also: though she kept looking at the lower lip, which after a while began to swell. Auntie was horrified. She thought about the pepper remedy once more.

But Goldie was still crying, the lip bulbous, out of proportion with the rest of her face.

Auntie moaned.

"If you not stop dat, you go be like one o' *them*!"

By "them" she meant the Africans who mostly lived apart from the Indians in the villages and districts along the tropical coastland. The latter preferred the towns, though Indians lived there too, many becoming *creoles*: their names became Christian-sounding, and they denied their Indian customs. The Indians ridiculed the Africans for having thick lips and large bottoms, and the Africans ridiculed the Indians, calling them "coolies" because they worked mostly on the sugar estates and planted rice. After a while, the ridicule became friendly banter; no one took it seriously, though there was underlying rancour. But where Uncle worked (close to the town), the Africans were his best friends; he often bought endless rounds of drinks for them; sometimes he brought them to the village, to our house: to Auntie's utter dismay, because this meant a feast had to be prepared, usually chicken curry. All the while Uncle's friends laughed heartily since they liked when she cooked roti, the flat bread that was a delicacy to the Africans. Auntie, of course, resented them, though pretending to be a good hostess. Now she was seeing in Goldie's face some of what she resented, the large, bulbous lip. She moaned.

Goldie, instinctive as it was with her, sucked the lip harder, then giggled. The rest of us, her age, ran around her and teased loudly:

"Suck Lip, Suck Lip!"

Goldie giggled louder, she liked being called that.

"Stop calling her dat!" Auntie bawled, really querulous as she'd become; maybe because now Uncle slept for longer hours, and all the domestic chores were left to her.

"Suck Lip," someone else jeered, out of Auntie's reach.

"Stop it! Stop it!" Auntie yelled, hands akimbo.

Goldie, in a corner, remained quiet–a smile on her movie-star face. And her lower lip curled in and out, slowly; indifferently.

When Auntie took off to the village market, we were at it again. Forming a small crowd around Goldie, we looked closely at her lower lip, and jeered: "Hey, Suck Lip, you t'ink you going become a movie star now, eh?"

Goldie smiled, as I knew she would.

"Come on, Suck Lip, tell we that, eh? Everyone t'ink you so beautiful. Heh-heh. You t'ink you really are, eh?"

Goldie laughed this time.

Once or twice, though, she seemed sullen; as if thinking about something else. Then suddenly she smiled again, undeterred, indifferent. And the lower lip was like an illuminated pink bulb which hung on Auntie's Christmas tree each year, the one she never threw away.

I asked Goldie: "Why you really suck your lip like dat,eh?"

"What?" she replied, churlish, shaking her head–as if retarded. She'd been sucking her lip for the past hour.

"Sucking you' lip?" I said, impatient, because now I didn't like the way everyone teased her.

Goldie shrugged; she didn't care. She blithely kept sucking the lip, her mouth twisting slightly, and so odd it was.

Auntie was now coming down the main road, her bag filled with small red crabs and tiny shrimps which would be prepared with spicy masala, the meal for that afternoon, and maybe the next morning. The next day she'd go back to the open market to buy fresh fish and vegetables.

She saw us huddled about Goldie, and she knew at once what we were up to. Her pace quickened; a scowl carved on her face.

Goldie's lip curled in and out, quickly, like rubber.

Auntie drew closer.

This time she didn't bawl out. To Goldie, only, she said: "Still doin' dat?"

Goldie looked around uninterestedly.

But by now Auntie had reached a point of high frustration. Pain was on her face as she looked at Goldie, then at us. Hurrying to Uncle's room, she cried out:

"Wake up, man. Wake up! Come see your daughta–come see!" She temporaily disowned Goldie.

Uncle growled in a sleepyheaded fashion. "What...now?"

"Don't you see?" Auntie raged, thinking of the size of Goldie's lip as I figured.

"See what?" Uncle turned reluctantly, to face her.

"Goldie!" she screamed.

But Uncle merely turned on the otherside of the bed. He'd been drinking a lot the night before; he didn't want to be disturbed. Goldie was far from his mind now.

Auntie gritted her teeth, and stood with hands akimbo, over him.

Uncle pretended he was still asleep.

Auntie growled and moaned loudly; such was her anger, frustration, her arms rivetted to her waist; Goldie's large bulbous lip in her mind. Ah, Goldie would never look like a movie-star! And...who would marry her? Who? The thoughts swirling, rankled her.

The moaning and growling and gritting of teeth got to Uncle. He got up right then. And it happened–suddenly–like something that was never meant to; something no one really thought would occur, knowing Uncle the way we did.

"My God!" I let out, when I saw Goldie again. "What happen to you, eh?"

Goldie looked pale, her face red, the lower lip completely swollen–ten times larger.

Goldie didn't answer; she seemed unable to talk.

In her eyes, though, I detected a dim smile.

From outside the house, we heard Auntie and Uncle bawling at each other.

"You want fo kill she, eh? Wha' happpen to you, man!" Auntie--raging. I'd never heard her like this before, as if she was in an immense torment, tearing her heart out. "Slapping her like dat, eh? Wha' happen to you, man!"

"It's the only way to mek her stop her bad habit," Uncle managed a reply, less loud, his voice weakening against Auntie's onslaught.

It was from that time on–as I recalled–that we stopped calling Goldie "Suck Lip." And, oddly, she seemed to have stopped sucking her lip.

Various versions of how Uncle slapped Goldie circulated. The one most popular was that Uncle, while sleeping, dreamt about what he would do, if the pepper remedy didn't work. Then, in a rage, unable to bear it any longer, he'd gotten up...

* * *

Goldie grew up looking really beautiful. I watched her all the while, the two of us getting closer. Real friends we were in a way. Then one day talk started going around that it was time for her to get married. Such were our East Indian ways; everyone wanted to protect Goldie's name. Of course, the parents had to arrange matters, to choose the appropriate husband. All the parents' work, the relatives' endless advice.

The suitors came around, all sorts, some riding by on their new Raleigh bicycle, their hair neatly combed with vaseline grease, which kept their heads shining, glinting in the sun. Goldie revelled in the admiration, though sometimes she seemed indifferent. Once looking at her, I saw the lower lip suddenly curl in, then out.

She laughed when I told her this.

I laughed too.

I concluded then that sucking her lip as a child had enhanced her looks.

She seemed as if she wanted to cry just then; it was the end of our conversation.

Auntie became the centre of things for a while: she scared away most of the prospective husbands with her relentless stare; she only wanted the best for Goldie. Verne, quiet-looking, and stable–he was the one. Goldie didn't really have a say in the matter. And all the relatives consented. No doubt they liked Verne's serious expression, made more serious by his wide-rimmed glasses.

Nearly everyone in the village came to the wedding, poor as we were. And Goldie, in white bridal gown, looked exquisite; no longer like the niece I'd grown up with. She looked like an actress of sorts. Auntie beamed as she watched Goldie: it was as if she was the one getting married. Uncle, well, he was in the far background.

I became unhappy that Goldie wouldn't be around as often as before. She'd have to devote all her time to Verne: the quiet, resolute type he was, the village politician–which Auntie didn't really know about at first.

Auntie looked at the wedding pictures over and over, showing it to the neighbours; then the endless talk about it. Once in a while, Uncle laughed, to himself: as if he remembered the day he'd gotten up in a fury and slapped Goldie.

My impression of Goldie going off to live with her husband was of someone smiling; politician and all that Verne was (he'd hinted about some travelling in the air). I looked at Auntie–who laughed to herself then once more looked at the wedding pictures.

I visited Goldie from time to time. Her first-born eyed me strangely, as if I was an intruder.

"Where's your fader gone to now?" I asked the boy.

He shrugged, this two-year old: a little like Goldie herself: nice little curls on the sides of his head.

"Where has he gone to?" I demanded, somewhat playfully, though still serious.

He shrugged, and ran away.

Goldie murmured, "He go soon come back, dat man." She meant Verne, and she looked at me, at how dissatisfied I appeared. "In a month's time," she added, dully.

"You shouldn't have married him, Goldie," I let out.

She smiled, indifferent.

"He should be at home wid you; you...his wife. This child needs a father at home," I said a little angrily.

She nodded, looking around for her son. Another child was on the way. And Goldie seemed rueful; even mournful.

She began talking about the past--always the past now. And about the time when we were children. She smiled. Not once did she mention the sucking of her lip. It was as if this never happened.

When her husband came home, handing her another woollen cardigan, he was forgiven. But he'd go off again.

To me, Verne was really a man of mystery. Yet, I figured he perhaps was important. So Auntie also felt; though she now kept away from him, from them. A few "important" people called to see Verne from time to time. They talked about trade union matters, politics; about the Party; other parties' names mentioned; other races, movements. Strategies and tactics. All vague, dull to my ears. Nothing about his son, or the new one soon to be born.

Verne took off once more.

I said to Goldie, "The two of you...you're so different."

She once more wanted to talk about the past.

One day I let out, "That man...he's a Communist!"

I didn't know why I said that.

Goldie looked alarmed. But then, her face was the same as before; hardly a ripple. She shrugged. And her sons badgered about her (the second was now born and becoming hyper-active). The first swore like a grown man, his finger-nails caked with dirt. The other gritted his teeth; both on the way of becoming full-grown vagrants.

Goldie looked remonstratingly at them. When they cuffed, kicked each other, Goldie yelled, "Stop it," her voice grating, like a mad person's. She reminded me of Auntie just then; I was alarmed.

"Stop it!" she hollered at her children again, her lower lip then curling in; and her eyes widened, swivelled; like a strange sickness taking over.

I thought I was imagining this.

A few days later, her eyes looked really bloodshot. And for the first time I noticed, too, how fat she was becoming. The fat appeared in rolls; elephantiasis had set in overnight.

"You should lose some weight, Goldie," I told her one day.

"What for?" she asked grumpily.

"For...your husband to see..."I argued.

"He doesn't care, he gone away anyhow."

"He sees other beautiful women abroad," I murmured, not sure.

It was as if Goldie understood me fully, and replied: "I *am* beautiful."

"Like a film-star, eh?" I teased, laughing.

She began to cry.

When her husband came home again and saw how fat she was, he let out:

"OH Gawd!"

But he appeared oblivious of her fatness, preoccupied with his politics as he was Each time he talked, it was to reform the country, to eliminate poverty and superstition. Goldie, in a corner, watched him as he added:

"The country must become modern. There's need for a genuine transformnation." He was speaking to me.

I didn't reply.

He continued, sometimes for a full hour; and I hardly got a word in.

Then he was gone again. Goldie, sighing, said, "Maybe he will stay away for a year this time."

"Maybe." I was still thinking about the things he said, about transformation; and each time he returned, he seemed even more fanatical.

Goldie looked bigger, like a tube or a barrel. Another time, she looked like a blimp.

She laughed when I told her this. The children, overhearing, also laughed.

"Stop eating so much rice...that kind of food," I berated her.

"Oh," she ignored me with a wave of her hand, turning away, fingering the Polaroid camera.

Her children growing older seemed a little more responisble (though still vagrant). One urged her to lose weight; they made fun of her when she ate.

But Goldie appeared thrilled–as she sat before her plate.

When Verne came home again, looking smart and handsome in jacket and tie, a tape recorder and other odds-and-ends tucked under his arms, he didn't comment on Goldie's fatness; though everyone was expecting him to.

"How's it...abroad, I mean?" I asked him at once.

"This country needs change. There's too much ignorance here. The people, I mean." His eyes strayed to his wife's body.

Suddenly it appeared to him how really fat Goldie was.

Like an explosion he burst out, "Oh Lawd!"

Laughter.

The children laughed the loudest. Goldie also laughed, as if the joke was really on Verne.

He looked at me; I was also laughing.

He reddened. Then once more he began talking about politics, his travels to Bulgaria, Yugoslavia, Russia. He made lengthy comparisons with the way it was there...and here. He'd visited all the Eastern bloc countries. Finally, with an almost wild gesticulation, he cried out:

"America's an imperialist country!"

Goldie seemed interested now.

"When will you go there?" I asked him, discovering irony.

He didn't answer. He was thinking, looking at Goldie's stomach; then, at her lips.

I too was looking at Goldie, and suddenly, as if this were a deliberate act, Goldie's lower lip curled in, heavily–like something she'd planned to do just at this moment.

Verne seemed frightened. He blinked in quick succession–as if what he was seeing wasn't real.

"Well..?" someone pressed for an answer.

"I...I don't know," he finally said, eyes still fixed on Goldie's lip; on her, entirely; as if she would become fatter that very moment and fill up the entire living room, and soon after the entire house, swallowing him up in the process.

I kept my gaze fixed on Goldie, on her lips curling in again, without indifference on her face. A suppressed anger which had been bottled up in her all these years was now breaking out.

Verne–sensing this–bit his own lip, fiercely; a reflex action.

I saw blood.

And when their quarrels started, I knew it was the beginning of the end.

# GOD SAVE THE QUEEN

I stood at the church tower, my familiar vantage point, and looked below at the darkwatered creek winding through the village; the leviathans were at it again–I felt–splashing, creating havoc. And the school close by where Mrs Grant–the formidable one–heaved hard, as if the entire creek, district, was heaving in her. Little did we know she was suffering from a strange illlness, her fat legs like tree-trunks throbbing; her arms, entire body swaying; though, at times she appeared subdued, soft. And we figured that no matter how silent we were, she heard us. My eyes turning to the stalwart *saaman* tree with wild orchids growing from its buttressed roots, sometimes suddenly bursting out like bags of blood. Then back to the creek once more, like an obsession: I watched with a mild awe; looking below at the main road, who were passing by, mere specks sometimes...Harry?

In the school again, Mrs Grant smiled, against a gust of wind on this sultry day. Now she led us into song, preparing us for a "concert"--as she called it--and it was as if we were all English, and it didn't matter if she was African and the rest of us were, well, East Indians. "Sing well!" she cried. "You will be the best yet." The school at her command, which in a way the old headmaster, Mr Thoms–the sleepy-eyed one–acknowledged. Mrs Grant always wanted the best from us: we'd one day match even the best in England (or America), or anywhere else in the world for that matter. And more lustily we sang "God Save the Queen," now that we heard Princess Margaret would be coming at our country's independence, hosannas in my throat, my own mouth opened wider, a false note no less! Mrs Grant's hand raised, conducting; then, a grimace.

The others nudged me at once; then their titters. But next our hallelujahs rose across the Anglican churchyard, the giant tree rustling, the orchids rampant. And Mrs Grant's hand was still raised, expression rigid. "You will be the best!" she cried. I started thinking of those who'd come to listen to us on "concert day:" the overseers and their wives–from England–and the other well-to-do of the district: the shopkeepers, their families, the proprietor of the local cinema–Mr Zap, we knew him well–and maybe a government official from the capital. Mrs Grant's eyes glinting on this special day. And Princess Margaret, would she really come? Suddenly, *whop-whop-whop*! I flinched–the pain racing down to my toes. The dreaded cane that she wielded–I smarted from the bitter blows. Instantly she was telling me to concentrate harder, sing better, if I could–I had to be the best!

The pain still searing through my body; and Mrs Grant looked at me, with pain all her own, it seemed. And I retreated high up to the church tower once more, like escape; my head spinning as I, oddly, kept recreating Mrs Grant's voice. But she seemed already gone. And it was Harry I saw: he, the derelict, on the road more than a speck now; the creek suddenly winding further in my mind's eye. The day dwindling, crepuscular light. The leviathans, gurgling, splashing about more than ever.

The next day I searched for Mrs Grant, but she was nowhere to be found. It began to be rumoured she wouldn't be coming back to the school. "She really gone," I heard, which I repeated in awkward tones. None among the other teachers knew where, and maybe they didn't want to tell: a collective sigh on their faces. And just then I thought that one day I'd also be a teacher like Mrs Grant, resolute, eager to make my charges learn...for them also to be the best! "Mrs Grant, she dead now," came the news. Was she?

A prolonged mourning followed; though some of us pretended not to mourn. And at home, I stared at the walls, imagining her still trumpeting fort, music in my own ears. A great soprano in a faroff place--New York or London–she was: there where perhaps she always wanted to be. But I also thought of Harry, the outsider, white-skinned, who'd come here as an overseer from England (no one could really remember when): and, maybe, the tropical sun had made him giddy, deranged: all attempts to send him back to England having failed! Mrs Grant perhaps understood what made him tick each time Harry laughed outside the door of the school, talking loudly to himself in the sun, swatting at invisible temperate flies (maybe) and swearing at the world. Mrs Grant singing loudly in London's Royal Albert Hall, her own hosannas, and now leaving us now here in the fierce's sun heat. Suddenly I cried out: "It good she dead!" I repeated this when the others came by: "It good, 'cause of the licks we used to get from she!"

"Yes," came a chorus, laughter.

"But she dead fo' truth?" asked another, like mockery.

I retreated into myself, thinking of the expatriate managers speeding by on landrovers, motorcycles. Acrid sugar cane smells in the air, molasses fumes rising, the distinct odour of our parents', villagers', lives. And the tombstones in the churchyard, derelict in places; other stones scattered amidst wild flowers, an assortment of ornamental bottles, other objects like emblems. The leviathans again, the creek endlessly winding. And the massive trunk of that familiar tree next, which seemed to anchor the whole earth now; the orchids more fully red, brighter in the sun's glare. Mrs Grant was now one of the orchids, I figured: she, reappearing, reminding me who I was; yes, I'd become a teacher like her one day!

"You're growing up fast," an elder said to me.

Another: "You will become a teacher, no?"

I nodded, more determined.

"Imagine you wearing collar-an'-tie!" It was as if Mrs Grant herself decreed this; the workers passing by, some looking up at the tower, eyes taking me down, my walking along the asphalted road shimmering in the heat. Long days, weeks, months: a whole year. And another; the orchids, cane leaves–like arrested fragments of the sun. Harry–"Stinker!"–laughing hard in sporadic rain, season after endless season. "Yes, you Harry!" the others called out. "Go back to England--where you come from. You don't belong here!" And my own voice, trembling:

"Yes, tell us where Mrs Grant gone, eh?"

The news was out, I had passed the Pupil Teachers' examination. Suddenly all my years of growing up seemed one bunched knot, rolled together. "You're a real teacher now," one said. "You'll be like her." *Mrs Grant*? "You know who we mean." A former classmate's voice, hosannas still in his throat.

I rode home on my Raleigh bicycle, the tower itself looking down on me, asphalt cracking, the road meandering. Harry, just as I expected, hailed me; but the kids–much younger now–yelled out: "Stinker-stinker!"

"Mad white-man!"

I pedalled harder. Harry's skin was now brown and blotched from his being too much in the sun. I pedalled on, going from school to home; the next day, and the next; and back to the same building housing almost five hundred pupils or more; though none such as Harry--the grown man that he was, with a child's mind maybe; sores on his body; unkempt, unwashed. Faster, as I kept thinking of him as an illiterate: so unnatural in a way, because of who he was. Maybe he'd be willing to learn: Mrs Grant once wanting to teach him in her fashion, with tender care, patience; and Harry responding as she asked him about England from time to time: at such times he laughed loudest, as if he knew what she was up to ~~her~~, her wish to go there.

I also laughed. Now I imagined Harry in heavy winter coat pulled close to his ears, a cold wind blowing in his face; Harry also huddling in a street corner, brown paper bags pulled closer to his mouth, eyes, face. And Mrs Grant close by–in New York or London–crying out, "God Save the Queen!"

The next morning the children in my class dutifully stood up, bright, cheery, greeting me. My own voice cracking, in mute ways. "Sit, class." "Yes, sir," came the chorus to accentuate their dutifulness. And now my role-playing guise: the endless repetition of tables, words; the fatigue of my too-much talking, teaching.

They tittered: they too were becoming fatigued, the heat sweltering, unbearable: we were experiencing a more than usual dry spell. One or two giddily laughed, then badgered, complaining with racial slurs, the kinky-headed one's verbal barbs against the other with straight black hair, and vice-versa. But in another moment all was forgotten; the innocent faces of these ten-and eleven-year-olds, smiling after a while. It'd go on like this day after day, the cane fields surrounding the villages like veritable enclosures, swaying as far as the eye could see in each new gust of wind. A mirage of zinc-white clouds scudding by; below, as far as I could see from the tower once again, the workers–parents–whacking away in the fields, their faces covered with soot from the burnt cane. So unreal, their own selves: like deformity; gnarled limbs, bodies.

To my charges I said: "Your future's not here. You've got to escape. Learn!" Mutterings to myself in a voiceless, voice-filled day and night. Disillusionment in the wind's eye; the rancid smell of rotten cane, molasses–intermingling once more. "They'll learn like you, huh!" a voice said, my own conscience in a way, questioning my motives...as the wind kept hurling, a saccharine-sweet smell in the air; the factory grinding, throbbing. Harry's face suddenly, pointing a finger, at me.

A parent's exhortation: "Teach them good, eh"; like a rebuke, yet praise. "They mus' escape!"

"Escape what?" I asked, in petulance.

No answer. Only mute voices in the hard sun. I stood before my class again, looking at their almost adult faces, their being unaware of the future or strange fate that awaited them. And why did Mrs Grant choose this school to teach...here where rice fields were reclaimed swamps? My eyes closed, thinking...it must be the heat. From the window the clouds coming down to the ground, as if to genuflect; the horizon at bay. Leaves scattered, swishing branches; other clouds scudding by as if on wheels; the world topsy-turvy more than ever.

Ah, I thought, Harry was the only one who understood everything--he outside all day walking, knowing exactly when a storm would come; he who talked to the dust swirling in the air, stumping his toes as he walked barefooted, the ground slowly sucking the blood out of him as his feet bled. Mrs Grant, I figured, was still keeping an eye on him, stirring him with new hosannas, hoarse as she'd become: she who could no longer sing loudly.

"You better learn," I shrieked to my charges in the bewildering heat. "Or you'll end up like...HARRY!"

They laughed at this harangue. "Why you tell us that?" They demanded an answer.

I relented, thoughts haywire.

"I want fo' work in the canefield when me grow up," one boy churlishly said. "Just like me father." A future's limit in his sharp eyes, his words' refrain. "Yes, me, too want to work in canefield!" a darker one said. "Yes-yes!" A clamour, further chorus. "Ha-ha!" The classroom's swirling air, intense humidity.

"No," I said.

"Eh?"

"Learn to read and write!"

"So we don't become like stinky Harry?"

"Yes...stinky ...stinky Harry!" they clamoured, the heat itself vociferous.

Mrs Grant, on the sidelines, grimacing, yet urging me on; she even wanted me to fetch a whip and to start flogging: the parents expected this in a fashion, didn't they? Now I vicariously lashed out, the stings of the body–all my own bearable pain. Syllables of the hard ground; the Canje road itself like ancestry, winding more and more; the tower's bend, as if suddenly pulled to the ground. Dazed as I was, I once more heard the parents' cries:

"We depend on you, Teach."

"Teach them well so they become docta or lawya in England one day."

"They won't go to America?" I heard myself ask.

Harry also asking, laughing in his manner. And everyone else also laughing, because he was looking at the girls in particular and telling them that retarded as he was, he knew many things. Incredible. Smelly as he was... They put their fingers to their noses because the stench coming from him was stronger than rotten cane. And one chaffed: "Harry, how come you know so much, eh? Because you is a white man?" And, "Is England where you really born? Stinker, foreigner–not living in a big white house, how come?"

The boys shrieked louder, then hurled at the girls in inimitably spirited taunting: "Who go marry Harry? Who?"

"No..no....NO!" shrieked the girls, covering their faces, bashful-tittering.

"Who?" the boys demanded vociferously.

"Dularie, Zeena, or Bibi...WHO? He'll take you to Englan'...or America! London or New York!" Voices, like an ancient truth, or mocking adults' eyes.

The girls now laughing heartily, they with women's faces. Nubile, full-breasted as they seemed. "Who will marry the white man?" And, "Harry go give you all belly!"

"NO!"

The girls' hair neatly combed in braids; the boys' plastered with white vaseline, combed straight back. Eager-faced they were: as I watched them before me. And once more we set about repeating arithmetic tables, numbers at my command, cane in hand. Then, loudly spelling words: the rhapsody of the three R's. Symmetry or rote, Mrs Grant with me all the way: "God Save the Queen!"

"You're doing well," I coaxed. "You'll have a good future–all of you–if you learn well!"

"When will I become a docta, sir?" one boy impudently asked.

"But I want to be a lawya," cried a girl.

"Gals na become lawya," hurled a boy. "Only hairdresser!"

"No!"

And someone else said, "Ask Harry!"

The sun became fiercer; the insects humming along the gables, eaves. Giddy we all were. Image after image, the previous night's: the factory throbbing harder, incessantly pounding, as I murmured: "You definitely wouldn't be like Harry," and watched them puzzle over arithmetic. One girl suddenly put her finger to her nose, pinching it as if to ward off Harry.

More of the sultry atmosphere, the scarce wind, the sun overwhelming day after day in a prolonged dry season. How I longed for rain, veritable torrents: large drops pelting down on the zinc-topped houses. The girls in my class, beautiful as they were, still awed by Harry: bedraggled, outside in this same wishful rain. Harry, windswept, drenched, hair splattered about his face, clothes soggy and about to fall off his body because of the lashing from the rain drops; Harry, eager for shelter, but there was no place for him to hide: his clothes actually falling off, skin now whiter–he was no longer smelly Harry!

Next he was exultantly running down the main road...Harry, shouting voicelessly. The others' loud cries: "Harry, you will catch pneumonia. You will...die!" Mrs Grant, looking over my shoulder, exhorting him to keep away from the heavy downpour, lightning flashing, thunder's reverberating peals. But Harry now stretched out his hands, like a supplicant: as if reenacting an ancient ritual. Next he was running about in a circle; dizzying, eddying.

"What's de matter, sir?" asked one of the girls, noting how odd I looked. Her long-braided hair, festooned with flowers; abundant hibiscus on the desk before her; our tropical ways with more waving hibiscus, garlands.

"You okay, sir?"

Laughter: despite the heat, the petals unfolding, greenish sepals quivering; moist stamens, firm, erect. One boy said, "The heat getting to he!"

"Yes–it hottest today," another said.

"It's a drought," I calmly replied, wiping perspiration from my neck. Yet my sense of imaginary rain.

They started putting more flowers in their hair, faces, necks, breasts: as in a wedding ceremony. One older girl came up to me and quietly asked: "You not feelin' well? The heat, eh?" Concern in her voice, her breast rising.

I nodded.

"Take us behind the church tower where it cool. Close to the cemetery, see–Mrs Grant now dead, eh." She laughed hard with prescience, mocking superstition.

The others heard her, clamoured for this.

"It cool there!" they pleaded, even more; the boys'laughter as well.

"But..." I began.

"We must," they chorussed. Flowers, their unfailing braids, the sun in their eyes; alphabets, syllables rushing out of their mouths. A few perspiring already, animated.

I imagined the orchids sprouting, convulsing outside. Creepers, a whole array, distinct from the tree: this greenery reaching everywhere; the tendrils curling, as if at any moment they would entangle, choke the lifeblood out of the large tree itself.

"You must take us there!" they urged, sensing I'd give in now... The pleasant breezes that often blew behind the church tower amidst blacksage, frangipani, acacia; leaves giving out distinct aromas so different from the acrid smell of burnt cane. Places to go, I kept imagining, thinking; to see really. The relentless humidity all along the coastland. The clamour of more children's voices; other teachers shouting, berating, or exhorting. Only we'd be at our best outside, lyrical in the air amidst the variegated flowers, fronds rustling, the strong breeze being all.

...We walked out in tandem, the entire class–as if acting out a fantasy. A few in front started running forward, welcoming a fresh gust of wind. "See, how wonderful it is!" a dozen voices let out.

...We walked past the large tree, as I looked up at the tower, my familiar haunt. But now the ground was staid, not topsy-turvy. The children began running, sprinting forward, close to the decrepit gravestones; some immediately splayed themselves out on the grass, leaves, fallen branches, logs. And the wind blew, a dreamful ease now as we started reciting the poetry of forlorn spirits.

We kept on at it while their parents toiled, grunted, heaving with the cutlasses, faces scarred, covered with soot. I began talking for their benefit of places faraway, England; the poetry of Cowper, Wordsworth; implanting foreign images in their minds. Worlds far apart, these lessons planned weeks ahead, which had been passed down to us...just as Mrs Grant had fashioned. Then–silence, the mute rhythm of words; further sensations, images. No other sound, save for the occasional bark, sputter of a motorcycle–like a distant raucous cry: an overseas manager's phantom presence. The trees rustling; the ground itself suddenly shrill, as never before.

"Our world, a much wider place," I started saying, asking them to suspend disbelief.

"Tell me trees, what are you whispering? Tell us of the past, slavery and indentured labour, the bones buried not far away. The cries of pain." I was carried away by history or heritage, the relic of thought, while the leaves continued rustling...Mrs Grant listening with a cocked ear. And spellbound they all were; bright new worlds, horizons.

"Yes, tell me trees, what are you whispering?" another chorus. One girl became tense. I looked ahead, taking in a thick cluster of blacksage. Zinc-white clouds again scudding by, as if in a hurry. A pulsation, somewhere as I studied the whiteness, snowy horizon, blue skies. No school bell rang, to call us in; nothing to break our separate reality and reverie as more leaves rustled; thickets breaking, cracking; insects crawling in a frenzy or turmoil.

*Someone coming*?

No, it couldn't be...no one else was here. Nothing supernatural in my mind. Just branches, yet leaves cracking. Days of slavery, days of yore. Mrs Grant, are you indeed here?

"You okay, sir?"

Who was coming?

"You sure?" This girl's eyes focussed on me.

An overall anxiety now; the idyllic air nevertheless, lulling me. We belonged here, away from the hostile sun. "You really okay?" repeated, like a benediction. I nodded again in more of the wind's whisper among the variegated leaves, sepia-brown, orange, emerald and green.

Someone stepping closer, a path broken, Mrs Grant among us, convincing us of further hosannas. A choir of leaves: "God Save the Queen." Princess Margaret indeed coming, her royalty's ways or travesty. Our tropical exultation. Step closer...fallen leaves; in the crackle and silence, one step at a time. Clouds still scudding by; insects humming, a bee planting itself quixotically on a flower and becoming glued to it, then with a sudden tremor, falling to the ground to die a noiseless death. Nature's concert of tragic acts, the comedy of silence.

Suddenly I saw him: coming from behind the large tree. Coming towards us. The class, still glued to me, my words. None was aware of him stepping lightly on grass, the fantasy of rain now over; he, almost coruscating in the sun's glare--naked!

I blinked.

*You okay, sir?*

He kept on coming, his hairy man's body. Lingammed. Or looming...the girls' faces. And I was willing them not to turn around; not to look behind.

The girls' hair bordering beautiful black and brown faces. In an odd way I started conveying to him--this one coming--with grimaces, expressions of outrage. *Don't come any closer--naked as you are*! Their parents still at it in the canefield, whacking away harder. A louder grunt in the unrelenting sun's heat.

How they tittered, laughed. But a few seemed anxious, maybe awed by my vague gestures. And the breeze blew harder, the insects whirring, a dozen wasps all at once zooming close to the blacksage. The sun itself now a giant wasp, whirring.

Harry seemed dazed, lulled himself. Unabashedly naked, all because of the torrid heat; or rain. His madness in a way, drawing closer. The girls' faces tight, innocence yet attractive: these fourteen or-fifteen-year-olds: before long they'd be dutifully married off according to prearranged Hindu custom. Flowers still hanging about their necks, garlanding time; the boys more animated with an incessant refrain of laughter, mockery: "Who will marry Harry? Who?" and, "Who will marry the stinker?"

Harry's face grim or dismayed. And no matter how I tried to will him away with more gestures, all frantic, he kept coming forward, the grass cracking louder now.

"You sure you okay, sir?" a dozen voices, the entire class, asked.

But it was as if I was mesmerized: still with Cowper, Wordsworth.

Laughter, now muffled.

Suddenly the words, a rasp from the back of my throat: "DON'T LOOK BACK!"

Mrs Grant, her voice ringing out, rebuking me for saying this damndest, most stupid, of things. And the entire class–all thirty of them–looked back!

...Harry, naked: standing there. An idiotic grin on his angular face. The girls' bewildered looks; their life-long innocence shattered like glass. Eyes, faces, their being absolutely spellbound, speechless.

...Harry, smiling, as if coming out of a daze. Hosannas locked in his throat.

"GOD SAVE THE QUEEN!"

The girls' lovely faces. Hibsicus, zinnia, frangipani. The giant tree in tremor; orchids bleeding. The tower, a real somersault; the entire creek tumbling with leviathans.

*For hours after I kept talking to myself, imagining further rain; Harry walking aimlessly, no longer a derelict but a man who'd gained self-respect. In these foreign streets: determined, though still desolate. And I was assisting him to find a place of shelter, telling him in no uncertain way he just couldn't live the life of a vagrant any longer. He needed protection from the biting winter's cold in London, New York...what did it matter?*

*"Stinker--you, there!" cried a new set of kids, all white-faced, fluffy-haired.*

*A few looking at me, pointing. At me?*

*Harry laughing, the whiteness of the snow falling on his blond hair. Mrs Grant, in a barely audible whisper: voice dried out; the children's own voices growing to a full realization of stranger possibilities...All that was yet to come!*

# THE PUJA-MAN

There were some things, of course, my brother would never do; not because he had any principles. You see, he went to whorehouses in the nearby town while his wife lay alone in bed; and he'd *backtracked* his way across the treacherous Corentyne River (not far from the Amazon and the Orinoco) to neighbouring Surinam in a small dinghy in night's stygian blackness (when he couldn't even swim) with waves lashing on all sides as the dinghy swayed with its heavy cargo of contraband–mostly engine parts–all of which he was taking back to Guyana; by now Guyana virtually didn't have anything: the inhabitants were actually starving.

He was also a brawler: more than your regular street-brawler type; more cunning, he often won his many fights. In whatever he set his mind to do, he succeeded. Now, when he said he wanted to come to Canada, I knew he would, despite the fact that the Canadian government was discouraging Guyanese from coming here on false pretences, swiftly deporting the illegals already here. Somehow, though, I figured the authorities would have difficulty with him, hardened as he was; there were things he had up his sleeves to surprise, even outwit, the best of them (I couldn't keep up with the many schemes flitting through his brain, when I was told about them by my mother–who was still there).

And before long he and his wife arrived in Canada on a visitor's visa. When they overstayed the time stipulated in their visas the efficient Immigration Department officials quickly got to them. I figured now my brother would try to evade the deportation order. He'd been expecting it, he said. Suddenly, though, he said he would comply. Canada somehow seemed to have brought about a change in him.

I wanted him to remain in Canada. But sponsoring him wasn't easy; there were too many hassles, bureaucratic red tape. He knew this, glaring at me when I visited him in Toronto (I was living in Ottawa, close to the bureaucrats: I knew their uncompromising ways). His wife also glared–eyed–me, though she was mutely quiet.

No doubt, the thought of slipping across the border to New York entered his mind. The more I watched him, the more I figured he was thinking about this. It was widely known among us that illegal immigrants thrived in the jungles of American cities. He–surely, wise in the ways of the world, with all his street-smarts–would survive. Now, though, he looked a little downcast, big and burly as he was. Yes, he really wanted to live in Canada...something about being here, the people being civil; once or twice he'd commented on this to me. His wife, Beti, was contemplative, moody.

The impending deportation was relayed quickly to my mother in Guyana. And as I imagined, she lamented, crying out as if there was a death in the family! Yes, she wanted all her children to leave Guyana--oddly, to be away from her. I imagined her consulting a Hindu-holy man who, over the years, had turned into a sort of clairvoyant in the way things changed for the worse in our village. Maybe she'd even do a puja, praying fervently, and still weeping. She'd keep doing this: such was her "devotion" to my brother. I also suspected that there was something in him that frightened her. The clairvoyant–whom she figured an expert–would consult all sorts of astrological charts in his pretence of "mystical" powers. Yes, this same one, the "puja-man" (as he began to be known), was also regularly consulted about births, deaths, the auspicious time for weddings; and invariably he charged a heavy fee, poor as everyone was–but it was a sacrifice that had to be made; maybe a religious zeal was overtaking the villages, country. Oddly, I too was beginning to believe in the "puja-man."

My mother, drying her eyes as I imagined, said to me: "That boy, how I want him to stay in Canada." Her tone was pitiful, abjectly mournful.

Another phone call to Canada, the receiver trembling in her hand: my mother now declared that the "puja-man" told her someone had *reported* my brother to the Canadian authorities. How else would they know where he was hiding?

Really?

My mother lamented, more distraught she became,saying that maybe it was one of his wife's relatives–there were many in Toronto–

who'd done this deed. *They had reported him!* She implied mischievousness to the entire group. With another phone-call, she declared that this treacherous thing was done by a male! The "puja-man" had told her this: he with all his charts conferring omniscience. He'd told her in almost precise detail (though not the name of the snitch).

The phone again trembled in her hand.

I immediately wondered about the repercussions this would bring about in the family; though I laughed a little at the time.

My brother took the news with a newfound stoicism, especially when he was known to harangue and bawl out as if a demon had taken hold of him. Now he simply looked at his wife, dourly; and maybe he was thinking that he got along well with all his wife's relatives, mainly the mensfolk: some his beer-drinking partners (I'd been keeping abreast of his activities). To his wife, though, he muttered: "Is just as I thought."

"What?" She was already sullen, she'd heard the news from Guyana about the "puja-man."

"It inevitable–we're goin' home."

"Home to what?" she snapped. "There's nothin' to do there," she lamented, moaned.

By now it was well-known that corruption was rampant in Guyana; every section of the society was corrupt. And maybe my brother was inured to this, because I'd once heard him mention Graham Greene's novel, *The Comedians*–though I hardly ever saw him read a book before. Yet during my last meeting with him in Toronto (the family members all around), he dwelt at length on Greene's views of the world: about Third World societies being inevitably corrupt. Haiti was the best example, he emphasized, looking at me, the "intellectual." I was amazed at his inciseness of mind.

When I frowned a little, he simply eyed me, as if to say that he too was educated; it wasn't only me (I was the eldest in the family).

"We must do something," he affirmed, not looking at his wife. He seemed inspired.

"Like what you been doin' before we came here," his wife snapped again, referring to his almost vagrant ways, the treacherous Corentyne river in her mind, the dinghy rocking, threatening to go under, high waves lashing on all sides.

My brother glared at her.

She softened, relenting. But the thought of my brother once more gallivanting with his many friends back there–many of whom were no-gooders–convinced her of a depressing fate ahead. And no doubt living in Canada for six long months had brought about a change in her. Deportation also meant that everyone would laugh at them–at my brother mainly (behind his back, of course).

His wife's continuing quiet seemed all.

I looked from one to the other.

Then, as if he was unable to bear it any longer, he muttered: "Maybe I should never have come here."

"But you–we–took a chance," she corrected. Now she'd become more assertive, to his face (the result of her being in Canada no doubt).

He looked at her, thinking, mulling. But once more the thought of being *reported* by one of her relatives gripped him; it made him angry, frustrated. I knew he'd been thinking of starting his own business in Canada; such was his drive, acumen and commonsense, he with all his worldly ways. He was bound to succeed. Now all that, those dreams, was dashed.

He lowered his head.

His wife quickly moved close to him; a sign of affection, touching his arm (though they weren't openly affectionate people). But this crisis was now bringing them closer.

"Ma said it was one of *your* relatives," he quietly accused.

"Don't believe in that puja-man!" she snapped again. "What he know?" In a way, she was appealing to his sense of disgust over religion, superstition, and my mother's overly pious ways.

He eyed her severely. "They got ways of knowing."

"Thousands of miles away, how they go know such a t'ing happenin' in Canada, eh!" she scoffed, more assertive. "This is white-people country."

"It make no difference; besides, it's about us–that's what he been able to tell," he replied dourly: not thinking clearly. "About your relative," he added next. This rankled her.

"Leave my relatives out of it, eh-man!" she snapped, again.

"They hate me–all o' them!" He was alluding to his formerly "treacherous ways" on the Corentyne river with the dinghy, which everyone freely commented on.

"Eh?" she shrieked, a rebuke.

My brother was resorting to his old self, which she could quickly tell.

"Is not true," she said, defending her family's honour, sulking, then starting to cry–easily lachrymose as she sometimes was; which was also a kind of defence mechanism against his wrath.

"How then?"

"How then what?" she dried her eyes, looking at him sternly.

"How they know?"

"Who?"

"The Immigration people."

She didn't have an answer, even as she kept looking at him half-accusingly and in feigned puzzlement.

Then, haltingly, she added: "We shoulda never have come here in the first place. We shoulda remain there...and STARVE!"

Melodramatic she was now: she looked at him more severely; as much as he studied her small hands, almost pointed nose. In a way, she often confused him; now it seemed she was getting the better of him.

He shook his head, disagreeing with her. "We woulda survive."

"Survive how?"

He waited, thinking...mulling. Then, "It bound to happen!"

"Wha' you mean, man?"

"Life in Canada...." He was being cryptic, even though he was normally straightforward, he--the plain speaker and man of action. "It's not the best place in the world here. You na see how it cold!"

They'd both complained about the cold; when it wasn't very cold, they still said it was. And they'd yearned, playfully, to return home to the sunny tropics, even if only temporarily. Like most people here, the tropics in our part of the world always seemed like paradise.

"It too hot there!" she snapped again.

Resignedly now, he said: "I know." It seemed he didn't know what else to say; he only watched her, a little askance; contemplating, no one knew what about.

Ah, they were allowed a couple of weeks more to stay in the country. During this time (as I found out from the relatives), my brother began to resort to his old ways: he started thinking of ways of escaping...of leaving his wife and running across the country, from Toronto to Vancouer, with the Immigration officials chasing after him, their really not knowing where he went after he left each city. Surreal images flashed back and forth in my mind, that Graham Greene novel, the inescapable Third World: how it was always catching up with us. And all of a sudden my brother was again crossing the treacherous Corentyne, the dinghy weighted down with cargo, waves lashing on all sides, water seeping in over the gunwale--the boat about to capsize in the night's pitch-blackness! And somewhere, gunfire. The Surinam military....No, it was Haiti! I woke up in a sweat...in Ottawa.

* * *

Next I heard him say he was convinced--such was his acumen—that the Canadians wouldn't send his wife home alone "to starve": they were humanitarian people. Yes, he'd keep trying to evade capture, he'd stay in Canada as long as possible: a new resolve. The thought of getting a lawyer had also passed through his mind, I heard. But he quickly gave up on that because he didn't have any money--he said loudly for all to hear.

His wife looked at little astonishingly at him; she knew what he was thinking. But...this was only for a while; because my brother once more resorted to his new-found "Canadian" ways: he was almost benign, passive; even obedient, willing to conform. When the two weeks were over, he'd simply allow himself to be carted off to the plane, he and wife–and be shipped back to backwater Guyana...to starve, die!

He became obdurately silent.

"What you thinkin' bout now?" his wife asked–she couldn't think of anything else to say; his silence bothered her (I was told).

"Nothing."

"Nothing, man?" scolding–because to her he suddenly was showing no initiative; in a way, she was starting to become disappointed in him; unconsciously–it seemed–she was willing him to resort to his old ways.

He nodded.

"You not thinkin' bout going back home, *to dat place, eh*!" She almost screamed out the last four words.

"Yes-yes," he snapped back, impatient, though he didn't raise his voice.

She shrugged, not wanting him to be angry–she knew his temper could be ungovernable.

Then, the other relatives came, mostly hers: brothers, sisters, other family members. They came to commiserate; they, oddly, suggested ways of remaining in North America, legally and illegally. Some said this in jest, especially the mensfolk; somehow they knew my brother and his wife would survive, no matter where they were. And, as always, everyone moaned the politics in Guyana. And yes–once more–my brother made reference to Graham Greene: seeing his current plight in the proper Third World context. Then some of the relatives said they too might consider going back to Guyana to live permanently...one day: though everyone knew this day would never come. After a couple of hours of talk about the harsh winter (a perennial complaint) and how lovely tropical weather was (always like Florida), the relatives, one by one, left.

Once more, my brother and his wife were alone. He looked at her. She, now resigned to her state, muttered: "I hope you not goin' to behave the same way you used to–when we return."

"What you mean?" He looked at her sternly.

She didn't have to explain: his question was rhetorical. And unconsciously she started thinking of the many nights he'd stayed out, leaving her all alone; and she, wide awake, wondering about him, where he was. Now willfull as she was, she continued, as if to herself: "You see how everyone else is here; how they behave. You see it on TV, eh." She'd watched lots of TV during the past six months, sometimes five hours a day, because she had nothing else to do (she wasn't allowed to work).

He glared at her. Then his look softened; he was thinking he'd no longer watch TV there (it didn't exist in Guyana); and maybe his view of human relationships, love between a husband and wife, had changed.

That night he kept thinking of his impending return; it preoccupied him endlessly, I was told. But anger was also boiling in him. And thoughts of the "puja-man" came back: he imagined our mother before him and telling him in detail who'd reported him, which of his wife's brother–unmistakeably a male! All my brother's old fears, anxieties, surfaced, all because of his impending return. And the faces of the male family members (his wife's) who'd left, their black humour, well-timed jibes: and he started hating each one; then–one in particular, who'd reported him to the Immigration officials! But no sooner the faces became a blur, male and female alike: though he fought to draw one out, the culprit; the "puja-man's" finger pointing.

His wife stirred–she was also awake. "What is it now?" she asked.

He kept staring at the ceiling, in the darkness; his thoughts fixed, nowhere. Then, he couldn't stand his own silence any longer; he replied, "The *puja...man*."

"Eh?"

He merely continued staring, the darkness all.

She turned to his side, facing him. "I done tell you, he not know anything." She was in command now; she half-lifted her body, across his: it was her way of showing affection, this closeness now between them.

"He does," he said, tightening his lips.

"Your ma, she shoulda know better; she shoulda never contact he." She waited, pressing against him. Then, "Is jus' like she–though," she scolded, taking liberties.

"Leave she alone," he raised his voice, even though his wife was almost on top of him, her elbow against his chest. The bed creaked hard.

"She got no business sayin' that to you," Beti added.

He waited, feeling her weight against him; he still kept studying the ceiling, thinking of the various relatives, faces in the dark.

She added, "My family–they only want to help." She took on an injured tone, waited, pressing more of her weight on him.

"Yes–by reportin' me!" Duleep raised his voice.

"Don't talk stupidness, man!" she chided, playfully yet determinedly.

"Eh?"

"You is me husband." This sounded like a new declaration. "How they could want to report you!"

He mulled over this; then he finally let out, laconically: "I know." It was as if he was bogged down by a deep-seated stoicism, and there were no more words, his thoughts unclear. He was shaken inside, afraid; yet all the while, he was aware of her closeness. Then again our mother's words, the frenzy and knotted web of her own emotion: and his past, all swimming up dramatically that moment before his mind's eye.

I discovered next that my brother had become a believer: he who all along often spurned all religion.

I imagined him humming a mantra, something half-remembered; which he'd heard my mother mutter in her private devotion...A few photographs of the deities placed upright against a wall in a corner-room, Ram and Krishna, others; his saying a short prayer, invocation....But also the darkness of the streets, where he was going back to, the tropics overwhelming, making him insignificant. And I couldn't do much to help him, because he was past the age required for me to sponsor him. Intercession on his behalf with the Immigration Department officials would be useless, they were an implacable lot. Next I imagined him drowning in the same treacherous Corentyne river, the dinghy overturning–on top of him, and he was bobbing, arms splayed out in abject helplessness...as I watched him finally going down, far down. And that same river was not in Guyana, but in Canada, not far from Toronto; maybe in Ottawa.

My brother started crying out, voicelessly.

His wife woke beside him, she tried to contain his flailing arms in the darkness–to calm him down. I was also trying to calm him down, my way.

But he ground his teeth; and his wife tried harder to wake him.

"What de matter with you, man?" Beti shook him harder on the bed.

He was perspiring heavily. Half awake, he looked at her: "Where are we?"

"Where you t'ink?" By now she was sarcastic, really resigned to their going home. "Is not Guyana!"

As if catching himself, he gasped: "The immigration officials...?"

"Yes–man," she said, determinedly.

"How they know to come where I was working?"

"You been workin' illegal–what you expect?"

"No one shoulda report me to them." He kept wiping perspiration from his neck; in a way he was embarrassed that he'd been flailing in his sleep. He said nothing else for a while.

"Is what you been dreamin' about, eh?" Beti asked, suddenly intrigued. She also wanted to laugh.

He only closed his eyes, tried to be calm, not to think.

This time Beti really laughed.

He opened his eyes widely, looked at her: and he was now unable to admonish her. But a slow hatred, greater than ever, was welling up: a hatred for himself because of his incapacity to do much no doubt, a sense of powerlessness: what Canada had done to him, I figured; now he was just a shell of himself. He felt a constant sharp pain at the pit of his stomach; and he perspired heavily (I'd visited them once more).

The next morning Beti said to him, "What was the matter wid you last night?"

He didn't answer; he only felt weak. It was like a slow drowning; he wanted to go back to bed.

"Tell me, man...I is you wife, eh!" She was ready to harangue a confession out of him.

She drew closer, sensing something urgently was the matter, the tension in his body, and she at once wanted to be affectionate (scenes from the soap operas she'd watched flitting through her mind). Next she embraced him, her smallness pinned against his large body (she was only five feet), her arms almost encircling him.

He didn't answer.

Then, "Was it the ***puja man?***" She was almost solicitous, though mocking.

He squirmed, turned away from her—peeling her arms away from his waist.

She laughed a soft laugh; which was still mocking in his ears, and said: "How could you want to live in Canada, grown man as you are, an' still believe in superstition. Is a good t'ing they're deporting us." She cackled a laugh; then once more she suffered an injured one.

In the next few days Beti kept taunting him, still with the same injured tone. He kept being plagued by his torturous feelings, so unimaginable before. At night, he slept for an hour or two, then he'd wake up instantly.

Beti would make as if to embrace him, holding him to her. Once she openly derided him: "Ah, we goin' back, to the *puja man*—back there!" and made a face.

"Yes," was all he replied sternly, though he also squirmed.

She made a face once more. Taunting, teasing.

Now all during the day, she tried to conjure up for him which one of the mensfolk (members of her family) had really reported him to the immigration officials. It was like a game; it was her way,in a sense, of getting back at him for all his past wrongs, the way he'd left her at nights and went out to whorehouses in the nearby town of New Amsterdam. Now in Canada he seemed completely under her control.

"We're really goin' back to the *puja-man*—to him!" she said, laughing shrilly.

I tried talking to him on the phone a few times; but he didn't listen--not for long. He seemed distracted. Now it was all between him and his wife.

Then, on an impulse—I heard—he wanted to phone Guyana, to find out details of the life there; as if it had been years since he left. But each time he was on the verge of doing this, he looked around first to see if Beti's eyes were on him.

"Is the puja-man you want to talk to?" she sneered, laughed.

He looked away from her, shrugging.

"Is no use," she said.

"What?" he shrieked at her, aggressive in his defence.

"Nothin',man," she laughed.

Finally he said, "I want to know."

"Know what?"

"Which one of you' relatives—"

"Is none of me relatives!" she fired back, almost as if she feared he'd finally come to know. And she looked at him, a little confused, because of the hardness of his mouth, the old self again. A slight tremor went through her.

Once more he looked at the phone, his mind in a daze; he wasn't sure what he was thinking; he wasn't sure about her as well.

She studied him, also not sure.

And once more thoughts of escape, in broad daylight: the images he conjured up: his being in the dinghy in pitch blackness, the choppy Corentyne waters one moment; then it was in bright sunlight, and he was steering expertly far away from the river police...and grinning. She looked at him, the expression on his face...the *puja-man* again?

He squirmed.

* * *

Now my brother carefully rehearsed his departure from Canada: everything he'd say, his last words, to each relative. Next, it was his being taken to the plane at the Pearson International Airport, a few miles from downtown Toronto. People everywhere, he saw, watched, the crowds: coming, going—from all over the world. Hundreds seemed to be coming in, smiling, happy. And more people—mostly immigrants, these ethnics—doing all sorts of work, tubanned Sikhs as security guards, confident, professional. He looked at them–and it was as if only he was being sent back home, deported!

The tall, blond Immigration Department official tried to unnerve him; unsmiling as he was, treating him as if he was a common criminal or a fugitive.

My brother was now being ushered into the Air Canada jet, his passport being handed to one of the stewardesses for safekeeping (so he couldn't somehow retrieve it and miraculously rebound onto Canadian soil); and the official's words: "Get the hell out of Canada!" Words clipped, yet firmly said.

But suddenly my brother responded, "What?" His voice was surprisingly loud, very clear: so that all the passengers heard him, those at the far end of the plane, all these mostly Canadian-born, travellers going to the sunny Caribbean for a vacation...to lie in the sun, bikini-clad, women, men–soaking it all up.

The image grew clearer in my mind: and my brother shot back: "I will, see. I have relatives, family here! In Canada...I belong here–just as you!"

The official was stunned at this insolence, this show of stubbornness at the eleventh hour. As if he was asking for a reprieve, yet defiant.

The official turned, uncomfortably, looking at each passenger; as if wanting their collusion with the immigration policy.

I heard his wife's voice: "What happen man, you not want to go back there?" Once more mocking: "You not want to go back to the *puja-man?"*

But he was unfazed, his voice clearer, playing his trump card: "See, my brother is here–he could, well, become Prime Minister one day!" And maybe just then he was thinking of the Graham Greene novel: myriad scenes, odd episodes, all bizarre, going through his mind. And the passengers, I figured, started laughing; they believed him, it was suddenly probable.

I felt uncomfortable, yet I listened to his firm, masterful voice. Ah, this way, I knew, he was having the last word: the very last.

The official was redfaced.

The passengers kept on laughing, as if the joke was now really on the Immigration department, the government of Canada. A heady spin, turnaround: all their already sunny faces, tanned bodies; as if they were all just back from the Caribbean: and were now on Canadian soil again...and my brother had indeed come back with them. They laughed harder, louder. And it began to seem that my brother and the official...were also laughing: all because of the *puja-man*'s tricks, I figured. Ah, I was now a believer also.

His wife, Beti, was saying: "See, as I tol' you so."

"What?"

"It's jus' as I told you."

"Told me what?" he barked.

The laughter in the plane stopped.

I was now shaking his hand, embracing him as never before; telling him with earnestness, that he was welcome, he belonged here--the Prime Minister that I now was in Ottawa.

Beti added, "You men, you're all the same." She shrugged.

The plane whirring, beginning to take off; and maybe the passengers were applauding my brother's compliance with the Immigration laws, finally. And he was reassuring everyone of his new ways, new self almost.

I waved.

The Immigration department official merely seemed to look around abjectly, as the plane rose from the ground: as if at that moment he regretted my brother leaving; it had all been a mistake. And he wanted to apologize, to me.

But it was too late.

All of a sudden my mind raced with new thoughts. And I knew exactly what would happen: once the plane landed for a fuel stop in Miami, all his former instincts, the old self, would return! This time he'd really escape, right before everyone's eyes–running away, dragging his wife with him; and she was running fast...with him. And they had planned this during the three-hour flight to Miami when neither he nor his wife–tense as they were–hardly said a word to each other...their thoughts truly hardened; they'd never leave North American soil! He'd never go back *there*; not to the treacherous waters of the Corentyne, the waves buffeting on all sides, the dinghy sinking slowly as he started crying out for help in the blackness of the night, and the river-police merely passing by.

Back in Ottawa, I listened to my mother on the phone, her voice crackling: reminding me about the *puja-man* once more, who'd predicted–she emphasized–that my brother would indeed run away.

Did he?

"Yes-yes, son," my mother's voice was pleading. "Or how else could he ever return to Canada?"

*But now it was really late...amidst a plane's drone, voices in the air, still crackling; and the breezes of the sunny south, the Miami palm trees swaying, a storm or tornado imminent; and my brother and his wife were still running away, he pulling her hard, her wisp of a body close to him. Their windswept faces; the rain coming down heavily.*

*...Snow falling, in Ottawa.*

# TWO

# JOGGING IN HAVANA

## 1

Going to some far and distant place, like a dream come true; and talking to one's self–also like a dream. A myriad place really; palpabilty with billboards displaying expressions of undaunted courage. Fidel Castro, Ché Guevara, other heroes of the revolution: all meant to inspire. The hard sun cracking, pictures faded, faces peeled. I balked at the message, the unmistakable flailing of the bourgeoisie, whatever was left of it in Cuba.

Hot, sticky. Now José Marti–the father of the Cuban nation–looked down at me, the billboards wavering a little. The entire Caribbean catching up with me: I was part of the North American delegation (scholars, artists) that disembarked from the plane; we were here to attend a special conference. I was also here to find myself.

Let me say that from early politics seared in my veins; the continual talk of transformation, our flailing colonialism, capitalism, imperialism; the Third World versus the First (why not?). I'd read Frantz Fannon, Marcus Garvey, Nehru, Nkrumah, Dubois: all in my inchoate dreams of liberation. And there was the Back-to-Africa movement: fellas all over the Caribbean changing their Anglophile names to genuine African ones, weird-sounding as some of these were. We'd also started calling each other "comrade," and committed ourselves in however vague a manner to scientific socialism. And how we argued for or against idealism, materialism; ideologies see-sawing in our minds.

I was chided for calling myself an artist. Was I for or against socialism? "The Third World doesn't need artists, but bread." "Without vision the people perish," I replied. "Bah!" A vague, half-muttered mumble of the phrase "socialist realism," unwilling compromise. Art for art's sake was bourgeois–never forget. Yet, Cuba welcomed me! Billboards wavering...our going deeper into the labyrinth of Havana. And images of Batistsa running the island like a large casino, teenage prostitutes everywhere catering to American decadence, no?

We'd extolled the changes Castro made; we applauded when he rebuffed the American Administration time and time again. Then, in Guyana, we were on the verge of a radical transformation ourselves after the years of British rule. But some were already becoming cynical: Would a Black government be any better? Are Blacks capable of governing themselves after the long years of colonial rule! Look at Africa...the corruption, authoritarianism, one-party rule! Idi Amin, Bokassa!

I–alone it seemed–dwelled on news about persecutions of artists and other intellectuals–the dissidents in the Soviet Union experiencing the heavy boot of Soviet power. The poets Yuli Daniel and Andrei Sinyavsky. Stalin's horrible legacy, trying to forge "engineers of the soul."

One morning I looked "comrade" in the eye and said I was leaving.

"To the Soviet Union?"

"No."

"Hungary? Czechoslavakia?"

Still no–those places were far beyond my ken; and maybe I was thinking only of America, Canada, the UK. I knew some of the "comrades" were being given scholarships to go to the Eastern Bloc countries.

But I was an artist...I wanted to be where freedom was all; where I could give full rein to the imagination. And, let it be known that my hero then was...Dr Slokan Charles. What would he say to my leaving? Charles himself was living in England, though from time to time he visited Africa, then came home and made colourful speeches which made front page news in the local newspapers. The "comrades" called him merely an "exile"; that was all.

Canada–not America or the UK–pulled me, a pristine place. It welcomed me with snow most of the year, though it wasn't reindeer and people living in igloos in downtown Toronto as I once imagined. Attending university, I felt Slokan Charles still looking over my shoulder. To the "comrades," I reassured them that we had to spread word of the revolution everywhere, including Canada. At the Lakehead, a northwestern Ontario town close to Lake Superior–I felt the onslaught of winter storms, heavy snow pelting. Later I found myself working in a giant wilderness park, Quetico, the scent of bear and moose in the wind. Ojibways, Crees; Ukranians, others; the Bee Gees. New friendships, old aspirations. I was still committed to transformation; I read *Granma* at the university library; the *New York Times, Washington Post, The New Republic, Harper's*, a host of other magazines and newspapers. I balked at the professors singing idealist praises–who looked askance at me for my Marx-inspired comments.

News of Dr Slokan Charles again: his novels began to be hailed in London and New York; his picture now on the front page of the newspapers in Jamaica, Trinidad and Tobago, Guyana. I also imagined him here on campus, giving a public lecture: talking about the necessity for progressive thought, scientific socialism.

Other students said I was an eccentric. I figured even the RCMP was keeping a file on me. Weren't they monitoring Third World student intellectuals, these "revolutionaries"? Student riots, sit-ins at universities. The Vietnam War. SDS. Jane Fonda rhapsodizing. The Black Panthers increasingly riotous....More than Mississippi burning!

"Read Slokan Charles, man," I said. Next I was talking on campus about the tribal kingdoms that existed before the white man went to Africa: before Stanley, Livingstone, Baker. Yes, and how Dr Charles was now writing a triology of novels based on ancient African civilization, about kings and queens whose deeds would make one's head spin. Charles had gone to Nigeria to lecture and do research.

But secretly I also wanted to ask Charles about my doubts, for him to put me straight about socialism: I heard of Soviet sailors showing their corrupt face once they landed in Halifax Harbour on Canada's east coast: Communism wasn't all it was cracked up to be. And what about Stalin? Eastern Europeans sitting on park benches in Thunder Bay talked forlornly about the past, cursing Stalin's name. And, maybe...only Cuba was the perfect socialist state.

In Ottawa, where I'd moved–to be closer to the action–I hankered after new experiences, new ideas. A Jewish New York-born professor, trained in Jungian psychology, whom I befriended–said I mustn't lose touch with the "tribe" (the place where I came from). Her thoughts whirled in me, as I kept thinking of the hot, steamy Caribbean on this coldest day of the year. Now the entire Caribbean was in turmoil: riots, shootings in Trinidad, an army revolt. Doc Williams had grown uncaring,unable to wrest allegiance from his people despite the abundance of oil. The rigging of elections in Guyana was international news. In Jamaica, violence amidst changing ideologies, Manley and Seaga trumpeting before microphones, rhetoricians and reggae galore. Bob Marley-Jah Rastafarai ascendant. Only Cuba under the charismatic Castro was stable.

Dr Charles was making fiery political speeches one after the other, unfailingly erudite. He was back in the Caribbean. And then Grenada, Maurice Bishop; more violence; Slokan Charles predicted invasion!

Deirdre, the New Yorker, made a willful corkscrew face as we drove past the American Embassy in downtown Ottawa. A swift illegal U-turn, and she cried out: "No one stops me, I've beaten the system!" I laughed with her in a kind of craziness, my thoughts still on Grenada. Later at a Governor General's hallowe'en party in Rockcliffe–Ottawa's east end–I listened to a Cabinet minister bellow "Gran-a-da." Comedy interspersed with heavy drama.

Deirdre said, "You're making headway," and muttered next about her childhood in NYC, and how often she yearned to return: memories of skating in Madison Square Garden as a child often came back to her. And how she much preferred teaching in America, if there were job openings. Looking fiercely at me, she said I should be living in San Francisco; not in Ottawa. Next Deirdre talked about America, a country with a powerful Bill of Rights–though most Americans didn't know it existed. One night she told me about her former lover whom she met in Zurich when she was a student: who used to beat her up. He was an Englishman; yet she was madly in love with him.

News came of Dr Charles organizing a conference of scholars and writers in Havana. Charles, you see, had now moved to the US. I was also beginning to a be writer. Yes, I'd attend–if only to see, hear him; to share in his new insights about socialism. Ah, what was yet to come. Gorbachev...perestroika and glasnost: a new Soviet Union or Commonwealth, reborn, revitalized? Wither Yeltsin?

## 2

Teachers, writers, artists, academics–at the Miami International Airport in transit to Havana. I started filling my notebook with ideas, sensations. Dr Charles's eyes sparkled when he saw me. "Ah," he said, taking my hand; after five years he remembered my letters, fan mail. He talked about his life, what transpired over the years. In his late sixties, his hair was greying considerably; tall, rangy, copper-brown, as ever distinguished-looking he was. He regaled us about a letter-writing campaign to the American Administration to grant the conference organizers permission to fly a charter plane to Cuba. He was convinced we could sidestep the ban. "Man, we worked blasted hard," he trumpeted. "We got fellas phoning the State Department everyday. They had to allow us!" His eyes gleamed; and then he looked at me only, as if saying–we are here now, aren't we? A propeller plane would take us to Havana that night despite sporadic rain, a thunderstorm brewing.

Tape-recorders whirred, Dr Charles kept on talking. "How could they not allow us intellectuals, artists not to go to Cuba? It's damned foolishness!" he cried in mock-rage, Caribbean-style. The way he enunciated, his dialectal lilt, cadence: all demotically charming. Yes, he was now an academic at Ilinois State University, teaching Black Studies–he said. He'd been on countless visits to Cuba over the past few years where–he declared–in line with genuine socialist transformation the races were equal. Unlike in America!

A young female professor from the University of British Columbia, Kaye–smallish, demure–drew closer to him, as if he pulled her like magnet. She was eager to know about his work, his views of other Third World writers–George Lamming, V.S. Naipaul.

Slokan Charles, upon learning she also taught graduate courses, with a surpised look on his face, moaned: "My dear, you look so young; like a child." It was his way of telling her a white woman had no business teaching Black literature.

Kaye smiled, she kept on being overwhelmed.

At about nine o'clock in the evening, Charles looked at his watch and moaned harder. Further anecdotes, his entire life's experience mixed with erudition, insights. Kaye, and all the others, revelling, lapped it up. I only watched him in slight awe.

He began talking next about Mayan culture. The world could learn a lot from the Mayans, many of whom were black anyhow, he beamed, his knowledge endless. "The Mayans had a unique agrarian system," he added. "Perhaps the most advanced, one which the Caribbean could do well to adopt. Let the Caribbean leaders implement what the Mayans discovered a long time ago, man." Kaye scribbled. "Then we wouldn't have to depend on the metropolitan systems that white people created. Let the European races continue on their own–we will pursue our own Black course!"

Kaye seemed mesmerized.

Charles said that in his novels there were endless allusions to Mayan agrarian reform. And talk about Cuba–once more–as someone sarcastically mentioned that Castro was white; he had no business being head of a Caribbean nation.

Didn't he?

Charles looked sternly at the speaker.

Others heckled: how dared this one oppose Slokan Charles?

"The Cuban revolution isn't to be turned back," Charles muttered, the veins of his hands purpling. "The class struggle–make no mistake about it. The race question would solve itself later." Charles looked at me, winked conspiratorially; then he started giving tidbits about the lives of the Caribbean leaders, beginning with Forbes Burnham of Guyana...all about the latter's wiles, corruption. "Burnham, that blasted fool of a man wanted to compare himself with Lenin. A Black Lenin!"

LAUGHTER.

Next, it was about how Eric Williams hadn't planned for the future of his small island. The way he said this, it sounded like a suddenly new fact. Then he moved on to Cheddi Jagan, the arch-Marxist of the region, whom he considered a true leader–because Jagan was blasted consistent. "You will see him in Havana," he said. "He's a genuine working class hero."

Next he lambasted the Caribbean Basin Initiative project very much in the news. "It's only designed to serve the rich, the capitalists," he mocked, looking around at his audience, at me, Kaye. And he talked slowly about Third World debt to American banks, all in the hands of the IMF.

"There should be riots all over the Third World to break down American institutions," someone muttered mindlessly.

Charles looked wide-eyed at the speaker, and dimly nodded.

So much anger was in him now, I thought, as his eyes burned.

"Comrades, Cuba is our model," he affirmed. But he was getting tired now, I could tell. Charles looked at me, muttered: "I'll go back to Guyana, after Havana; I should be in touch with my roots." Deirdre in my mind: New York City, skating down a wide rink in Madison Square Garden.

Charles smiled–as if he understood my own sense of self-exile.

Then he showed us a small collection of poems by an obscure Black Caribbean writer with an indigenous African name–telling us the poems were masterpieces; and the publisher–as I glanced across him and noticed–was in the Soviet Union. He insisted we should control our own publishing outlets; then Black writers wouldn't have to go hands and knees to white publishers in America to get their works published. Yes, Castro's Casa de las Americas was the real cultural center of the Caribbean. There we'd get our books printed!

He grinned, as if suddenly he didn't believe what he just said.

But everyone else nodded in agreement.

Why was I becoming slowly disillusioned, I didn't know. The rain started pouring; my living in Canada all these years and realizing the extent to which my life had changed. And Slokan Charles was suddenly appearing unreal the more he talked.

"Isn't there a dictatorship in Cuba?" the previously unfriendly questioner asked.

Charles scoffed.

I recalled my first meeting with Slokan Charles, in Georgetown--a serious teenager as I was then and thinking of writing as a career. Charles was giving a lecture on Conrad's *Heart of Darkness*, convinced that Conrad was a racist. The Black activists, all dashiki-clad from the US attending the conference, were pleased–for Conrad was a white writer, and all white writers were imperialists! Unplanned, unrehearsed, his lecture seemed. After, the handsome Slokan Charles–young and vigorous–started making passes at a leggy young East Indian hostess, one of many whom the government hired for the occasion, each thoroughly creolized. The latter smiled encouragingly at him, as if *told* to do so.

With a taperecorder in hand, I asked Charles how he wrote, what his writing habits were. A typical interviewer's question, I figured.

Swallowing a mouthful of beer, and still eyeing the leggy East Indian hostess, Slokan Charles put an arm avuncularly on my shoulder and said: "Boy, Mannie, writing's like fucking. You do it when you feel like."

We now heard the pilot's announcemement: our prop plane contracted from Pompano Airlines was ready to leave. The storm had abated. But another pilot, apparently, quickly said it was still unsafe; there was no need to take risks. And Charles continued to hold forth. It was 11 o' clock, and some of us were really getting tired. Impatient now, nerves raw. Yet Charles--as only he could--kept us excited, we were cracking up at his endless jokes–he, the master raconteur! But he grew serious again, saying we must distinguish subjective reality from objective truth, the dialectical way; only then we could make the proper class analysis. He lamented the fact that too much Western thinking was cluttered, unclear: North Americans weren't allowed to understand scientific socialism or the concept of the dictatorship of the proletariat because there was always a Communist witchhunt in America.

He added, "No serious intellectual debate ever occurs in America, because of this fear. Don't forget McCarthyism, comrades!"

Again he looked at me; and Charles kept transporting us all back to the Caribbean in no uncertain manner. Then, as if suddenly more nostalgic, he talked of the Corentyne coast of Guyana, which was occupied mostly by East Indians–the children of indentured labourers. Charles had set one of his novels there: he'd even lived there, if only briefly, and now–the beauty of the place sang in his veins, the Atlantic bordering an unbridled stretch of beach, swaying palm trees. Only speaking to me it seemed, he declared he was writing another novel set there. "I grew up among these people," he added cheerfully. "You see, the Corentyne is God's own Elysian fields." He laughed, his veins truly singing with romanticism.

I thought of the backbreaking work of the poor people there who eked out a bare living (my father was born and raised there).

Slokan Charles kept up the rhetoric, rhapsody: "Sir Walter Raleigh gave his life to find such a place; El Dorado is really situated there, comrades." When his eyes gleamed, he seemed transformed into a courtier, a black Sir Walter: tall, rangy, imperious-looking. Moira, his young American wife—we were introduced for the first time—came closer, her eyes also gleaming; while Kaye tittered, then retreated.

"In El Dorado, the king bathed in gold dust," Charles added. "The streets are paved with gold, houses made of gold. God, you ever heard of such a thing?" He was still looking at me. Then, in sing-song dialect he added, "Yes, de blasted place is de best pon dis God's earth. You goin' to return there, like I mean to—that same special place! People there truly enjoyin' the best, comin' an' going as dey please. It's not like North America wid its severe winter cold that we forcing ourselves to live in!"

Heavier rain falling, lashing everywhere. Trees, houses, being hurled more than the imaginary: everything pulled away, dragged by a fierce wind. At about one o' clock in the morning, the pilots said they were finally ready to take us to Cuba.

Slokan Charles was scheduled to give the feature address at nine o' clock that morning in Havana at Casa de las Americas. An international audience would be awaiting him, yet so far he hadn't slept a wink, and so hadn't we: the group of about twenty.

Against the buffeting storm, the pilot and co-pilot in the air argued about whether they should turn back. Lightning flashing: my heart in my mouth; it was like being in a bizarre collective state of mind: this moment, hour.

We arrived in Cuba half-tired, half-asleep. The José Marti International Airport welcomed us with cocks crowing; soldiers languorously moving about, rifles in hand, eyeing us surreally, smiling. But Cuba at five in the morning suddenly galvanized us. Billboards wavered, José Marti's eyes all along the road to the capital. We booked in at the Havana Libre (the former Hilton).

Charles said, "I think I will now go for a jog." You will? "Man, you're back in the blessed Caribbean. Enjoy it while you can." My thoughts on the people we'd seen on the way ("All men are good save those who do not work," José Marti wrote), the proletariat sugar cane cutters straggling along.

An image of Charles jogging, breathing in the fresh morning air, the sun coming out, singing in his veins. An Orpheus he was, imagined: maybe reflecting on the speech he'd give before long. Would he mention what I'd recently read about Cuba, details of human rights abuses, people put in psychiatric hospitals for trying to thwart the revolution.

Charles jogging along the seawalls, his young, beautiful brownskinned Afro-American wife beside him, their strides eating up the landscape, passing more sugar cane workers going to work through this portion of Havana: these "revolutionaries"–who no doubt were thinking of one day living in Miami: Radio Marti blaring out bourgeois music, rhythms distinctively Latin and Black, the sounds of Motown filling the air.

I closed my eyes to catch a wink, Charles' feet pounding in my brain. Next the Soviet Union, Cuba–walked in me; the sun fully rising across the Caribbean sea; Slokan Charles gesticulating animatedly as the morning's main speaker, declaiming that transformation was inevitable because history had shown us all the evils of capitalism. And no one--absolutely no one--should trust capitalism (glasnost or not).Indeed, Cuba must stand alone!

I twisted and turned. Charles' feet thumping, his breathing in the sea air fully, his face pinkish red; vibrant. His wife smiling.

The microphone throbbing.

## 3

President Fidel Castro himself would be addressing the conference. At last I'd see the real hero of la *revolución*. A wide grin was on Charles's face–so fresh he seemed–seated next to the Cuban Minister of Education at the headtable at Casa, and beaming like a schoolboy. Hush-hush; hints of security problems if Castro indeed came to address us. Wasn't the CIA trying to bump him off?

Castro's energy, all his irrepressible gesticulations–a cigar dangling from one hand or lips–telling us what Cuba was all about. This would be the immediacy, palpability, I longed for. Would he really show up? Charles smiled wanly.

Later I asked a tour guide to show us where Fidel Castro lived (I was accustomed in Ottawa to showing visitors where the Canadian Prime Minister lived on Sussex Drive, not more than a ten-minute drive from my home; and in a trip to Washington, I'd also visited the White House).

The moustachoid guide was no longer congenial. I'd definitely asked the wrong question. To my other questions, he gave only perfunctory answers. Then he added that many Cubans left for Miami--the convicts, criminals--because they were really the riffraff, reactionaries; and the revolution had no need of them; and, you see–let it be known–in the Soviet Union they would have been sent to Siberia! Yes, Cuba was a far-advanced socialist state. Ironically, he pointed next to the old Spanish architecture we passed, the legacy of Spain, residual colonialism!

Back at Casa, the conference site–a Black American folklorist-cum-poet, not impressed by what he saw of Havana so far, fatigued by the humidity and frustrated by the slow service at the shops (he couldn't find a decent postcard to send home to his wife in Ohio), went to the microphone.

"Could you tell us what is the rate of social mobility for Blacks on this island?"

The Minister of Education at the headtable smiled, his attempt to neutralize the questioner, though he also appeared worried.

A South African-born, Montreal-based academic who devoted himself to Black liberation around the world, hurried to the microphone to apologize to his Cuban hosts for the question asked by his North American colleague.

But the folklorist persisted in getting an answer.

Tension rose in the air.

"Blacks everywhere are in inferior positions," cried the folklorist. He wanted to know why.

The Minister of Education kept on smiling, even when others insisted that the question be answered. Then he said: "In Cuba there's no separation of the races." It was only upper or lower class. There was no colour bar in Cuban society such as in America,or other parts of the capitalist world.

A woman academic–also Black, from Albany, New York–heckled. "What about the gender question? Tell us how women are doing," she cried.

The Minister of Education muttered he didn't understand the question, the translation was too poor. He looked genuinely nonplussed, bewildered.

Slokan Charles whispered close by, a few feet away from me–"Man, that cat's asking an American thing; he's not a socialist. He doesn't understand the Third World. It's a blasted bourgeois question." He was referring to the folklorist.

But for a while the word "mobility" hung in the air, throughout the conference. Later, I would recognize real mobility at the fabulous burlesque, *La Tropicana*, which all Cubans were proud of. But there was no thought of that now: only the words of the Minister of Education as he repeated that no one–absolutely no one–should *racialize the class question*!

I tried to look at Cuba afresh, hoping for startling new ideas, new truths about socialist ideology, politics. The "guide" at our table over lunch quietly answered my questions, though saying nothing about Black mobility. He was simply an interpreter of the Cuban revolution. But we were keen on finding out more. More?

He was unfailingly affable, courteous.

He said he'd never travelled beyond Cuba, though he'd been promised a trip to the Soviet Union...about three years ago. Didn't he want to travel to America? To see New York City–what it was like? What did he think about the lack of freedom in Cuba?

The last question didn't surprise him, he said; but in Cuba there was freedom from lack of hunger, fear, ignorance. These were the essential freedoms.

I knew the line well.

I prodded my fork into a juicy papaw, swallowed a slice whole without chewing.

Why didn't he leave Cuba for Miami like all the others?

No...he was happy here–he didn't beam with a smile. You see, he assured me, he didn't want for anything; and, *compañeros* (he called us), there were reports of many Cubans coming back to our island because life in Miami, in America, failed them. It was a dog-eat-dog society, and the dope, gambling, unemployment, alienation...it was too much for them.

Rice, fish before me. Ah, he personally didn't care for the abundance of consumer goods; one endured the inconveniences–if such. Sacrifices had to be made to safeguard *la revolución*. Did anyone forget the Bay of Pigs invasion? Kennedy and the Mafia? And Marilyn Munroe? Cuba was playing its international role by aiding other heroic peoples around the world in their struggle against imperialism. The Nicaraguans. Angolans...he looked at me, daring me to disagree.

I swallowed hard, a lump in my throat; a cry in my heart.

That evening, a taxi ride to the north end of the city: a group of us in a Lada, so ubiquitous in Havava. We sipped *mojito*, watched young Cubans in amorous postures, a tall black youth clinging to his slim, attractive, white girlfriend–they didn't seem more than sixteen or seventeen. (*Do not racialize the class question!*) Later, we leisurely began the long walk back to the Havana Libre in the balmy night air, Radio Marti sounds blaring out at the seawall, listeners everywhere. Hundreds in the streets, sauntering, idling. A cinema close to a busy restaurant, a small crowd milling about. Two Southeast Asian youths--I noticed–forlorn, doleful, kept looking around. Were they from Vietnam or Korea? Students? What were they thinking?

Smiles.

Broken English.

They were far from home, and weren't sure now if they were students or simply visitors. Cuba was exciting in the beginning, but not any longer; they wished there were more people from the Far East here. What did they do in their spare time? They laughed, pointing to the cinema, to the old American movies,the billboard, *Duelo de Gigantes* (Duel of the Giants).

Kaye, relaxed, jovial; glad to be away from the Conference for a while. Another academic, Ron, said we were now seeing the real Cuba.

Kaye, more talkative, convivial; her eagerness to know and feel everything matched mine. Another academic, Burt, who taught Canadian Literature in Western Canada, was also talkative, the *mojito*, Cuba, doing this to us. The night air seductive, a cliched balmy breeze all. Two Cuban girls, one jet-black,the other mulatto, drew closer; beautiful they were, inviting smiles. *Pesos*, they said: Would I go home with them? They needed *pesos* to buy...what? Underwear. The ones in the shops were out of fashion. They also needed new clothes (which were awfully expensive in Cuba). Yes, I could come home with them.

Not to my hotel?

Ah–they were forbidden to go there. But they'd wait for me in the street, a block away from the hotel, if I changed my mind. Maybe I could bring a friend along. I recalled one academic earlier showing me a pair of condoms he always carried in his wallet.

Closer to the hotel, I turned around, and one of the girls immediately waved–as if willing me to change my mind–in the balmy night air, in free Havana...the seductive smells of this former colonial town redolent of Spanish galleons being sunk close by, pirates ransacking an entire island. Blood pouring out from large wounds, women screaming–raped! Batista, not so long ago...now these girls, eager to be better dressed, who wouldn't come near the Havana Libre.

"You see," said Burt, sipping another *mojito* with me in the penthouse bar of the hotel, "this is the real Cuba, the real Caribbean."

Kaye muttered, "It defies understanding that in such a socialist island there'd be prostitutes."

Some of the others at the Conference walked in and out of the smoke-filled bar. Where was Charles? It was getting late, and he wouldn't want to listen to hypnotic Latin music or watch young Cubans discoing the night away, as if a kind of defiant decadence had overtaken their spirits. A longing to be truly free! Maybe Slokan Charles was already sleeping, getting enough rest so he could rise early the next morning for his ritualistic jog. Exhilarating smells in the air; molluscs and seaweeds; a strangely perfumed gust of wind. I sat close to the window. The two Cuban girls I earlier met still looking back at the hotel.

Music throbbing. My own visions of sexy underwear, a fantasy of love-filled tropical nights, lingering.

Kaye sipped her drink. Almost chaste, pure, the way she sometimes looked. Burt also looking at her, Latin rhythms pounding, the further hypnotic spell of Havana: buccaneers and pirates, Spanish galleons tumbling in a stormy sea, or resurfacing in a skull-and-crossbones' life with compelling historical immediacy.

Was it really the *mojito*?

Kaye smiled, thinking of her New Democrtaic Party husband in Vancouver perhaps. Would Canada ever become a socialist country?

Across our table a couple of Cubans passionately kissed.

The portly waiter with genteel manners refilled our glasses, curtseyed, returned a few minutes later with our bill. Only American dollars, *por favor!*

Kaye and Burt got up to start dancing.

## 4

Why did I then begin to feel free as I never felt before; I suddenly wanted to discover something new, saunter along at my own free will. The torrid weather, immense heat, asphalted streets sweltering. But I didn't want to stay in the hotel any longer, to listen to the abstract talk at the conference.

I walked on, going somewhere; nowhere. Places in my mind, all of Havana in unrelenting waves, heat. I figured I could easily pass for a Cuban; just as much as I could have passed for a Mexican. Typical Spanish-styled buildings painted white, quietly ornate; they looked different in daylight. The workers in the streets, these proletariat (united with the working class the world over), kept up a mind-defying rat-tat-tat with their drills, like sporadic gunfire. Road-building work consumed all their energies, muscles tense against the earth: rocks, sand. It was a scene that could easily have been replicated in any North American city.

I sucked in the dry air, walking faster, thinking of the hundreds of vacationers at Veradero Beach...just two hours away by bus.

A strange unease seethed in me.

I wiped sweat from my face.

Where would I go?

In free Havana, all the myths of socialism before me; and I stepped in the direction of *La Universidad de la Habana*. Gigantic, but majestic stone steps leading up to its doors, my eagerness to be with the young all of a sudden. But the campus was desolate, save for two austere-looking women: like nuns without habits; who walked up the massive steps alongside me without even breathing hard.

Then they hurried on.

Graffiti on campus billboards; my searching for words of protest...iconoclasm; same as I'd find on any campus in a North American university. It started raining heavily; it was as if the world suddenly began weeping.

I huddled in a corner under the broad leaves of a cluster of palm trees and tried to imagine what was being taught here, classes on José Marti (the same Minister of Education who'd addressed us earlier planning all of them). Other courses on the poetry of Nicolas Guillen, Pablo Neruda, Salvador Allende; one on the Nicaraguan people's struggle against imperialism. Countless other courses on Marx and Lenin–all pointing to inexorable social transformation. Maybe there'd also be a course on Hemingway–he, the "revolutionary," despite his bourgeois preoccupation with bullfights, boxing, women. Plentiful images of an old man confronting a marlin at sea–a heroic socialist struggle, world revolution.

Hostility in the air; my sense of foreboding, gloom. I drifted into the *Museó Napoleonico*, eager to test my senses. Two matronly-looking attendants, one black, the other white (such equality, mobility), smiled; today, I was the only patron. The museum bare, the artifacts seemingly nondescript. I studied the two women, this attempt at mixing the races more than in equity...the mestizo concept; races were only historic inventions, Charles had said.

And the Minister of Education in a moment of heat had said that America was the most brutally racist of all societies because of its experience with slavery!

It grew unbearably hot as I walked southward along Avenue Salvador Allende, passing more restaurants. Eyes carrying me along; I moved in a northwesterly direction, closer to the bay along *la calle San Lazaro*. The heat more unbearable. I started looking for another musuem, any place, to escape the weather, Cuba. And how I longed for the winter's cold of Canada: repudiating the Caribbean, my roots, all my traditions.

A cinema loomed ahead. Something happening: in the lobby, older people walking about, well-dressed; a sense of busyness, purpose. My curiosity greatly aroused, I wanted to know what was going on. Was it simply the excitement to see a film?

I drew closer, circumspect.

Smiling, I entered.

No one taking notice of me; dark as I was, a Cuban, one of them. Yet I was anxious, apprehensive.

Those present were dignified-looking; no ordinary Cubans these; and suddenly I didn't feel free anymore. I looked around at the faces, expressions. A heavily built man, lightskinned, at the reception desk--cast a dark stare at me. Then he looked back at his pile of papers, membership cards. His chit-chat with the others coming in resumed. A middle-aged couple walked by, and he politely, deferentially, nodded to them.

I followed the couple, walking straight past him.

Words, mutterings in Spanish. My heart beating faster. I assumed an air of confidence, my guise intact: my really being a foreigner, or intruder?

The security guard at the desk again looked at me, then shifted his attention back to his membership cards.

I held my breath.

The guard lit a cigar; he seemed unsure what to make of me, who I was. About thirty people were now in the lobby, embracing, talking in subdued, yet animated, tones. A little inside the auditorium a few yards from the lobby, I saw about a hundred people (members) seated. And giant pictures of Castro hung in front, and one of Ché Guevara, on a wide banner that sagged slightly, words indicating that it was a special meeting of the Communist Party of Cuba. The word "*communista*" vibrated in the air. Everything grew officious.

My heart throbbed. I was an intruder, I had no business being here; yet my pretence at being...a delegate. I remained rooted. Here it was cool; outside, boiling hot. The burly guard got up from his desk and looked pointedly at me.

I hurried into the auditorium and sat next to an innocuous, austere-looking woman somewhere down the middle, near the aisle. I studied the other delegates coming in. The headtable began to be occupied, solemn-faced men and women, very determined.

The woman next to me appeared crumpled, like a crow. She muttered a word...something, in Spanish.

I didn't reply.

Maybe she was exchanging a fraternal socialist greeting. My fears of what I'd heard about spies in Cuba...would they mistake me for one? Throw in me into a Cuban jail in Oriente Province, and no one would know about it? No one at the Conference, not even Slokan Charles?

She offered a smile.

I kept my eyes fixed on the banner, the letters, Castro's eyes on me. Concentrating harder, I reflected on the fate of the revolution and the rumours of real changes taking place in the Communist world. Was it a meeting to decide Cuba's future?

Castro and Guevara continued staring at me–only. A few people: right, left, now looking at me. Some turning around. One frowned.

Once more the crow-like woman muttered something else and looked hard at me. I smiled again; but no reply. And I was also telling them in my stolidly mute way, *Look here,comrades, I've always been a sympathizer, which is why I am here.* I was also telling them about what was taking place at the Conference; and maybe Fidel Castro himself was speaking there now...Didn't they know? Or was Castro coming here instead?

Once more my heart throbbed.

Would Castro tell his select audience, all the party faithfuls, that he disagreed with revisionism, pragmatism? That in Cuba things were very different: objective and subjective realities being not the same as in the Soviet Union (or in America). Fidel–gesticulating heavily, chopping the air, spittle flying like sparks–remonstrating Moscow, the entire Eastern Bloc, telling them that Cuba's socialist path was different...there'd be no turning back! And absolutely no one could turn back the clock, could change the shape of Cuban socialism!

(APPLAUSE)

My thoughts topsy-turvy; an uncompromising but still charismatic Castro all. And was I in solidarity with them? Was I? Maybe not...comrade, maybe I was a revisionist.

Well.

The woman next to me tightened her lips. Her eyes seemed as if they would jump out at me. She pointed, at me–and she spoke quickly, loudly, a clatter of Spanish words. The entire gathering of delegates now turning back, looking...Who was I? Words in Spanish everywhere jabbed at me.

"*Pelicula, no hay*?" I mumbled a defence; it was a movie here,wasn't it? "No, eh?" I feigned a great innocence. It was also very hot outside, didn't they feel it?

"*Es verdad*?"

Quick, snappy questions, replies; more jabbering of words. An endless raising of eyebrows. I was being ferreted out, accused. Unnaturally clipped English next, then Spanish again; and the burly man at the desk loomed up in front of me. Three or four other guards (I didn't know where they came from) grimaced. Then it seemed an entire crowd was converging on me; and there was no air to breathe, I was suffocating. The crow-like woman laughed. Castro and Guevara looking down at me, asked: *What are you doing here*? *You*!

"*Pelicula*?" I muttered again.

Castro's eyes....No, no! A speaker at the microphone, in front, his words booming. A heavy hand fell on my shoulder. Get out! GET HIM OUT! Other hands, fingers pointing to the door. OUT!

*Compañeros*, please, I heard myself pleading, mutely; looking for a respite.

OUT!

Thoughts of my being in a prison once more; being somewhere far away from Havana, such as Oriente Province, locked up in a small cell, with barely a bed or bedpan in it. And no one would really know...for days, weeks, I'd be kept there. And I was telling my captors it was a genuine mistake; I really wanted to listen to Comrade Fidel himself at the Havana Libre (I was part of the North American delegation, remember?). I was, believe me, a poet ..from Canada. Many Canadian tourists come here each winter, eh?...Veradero Beach, comrades.

## 5

Images of an Oriente Province jail remained with me, my tormentors still with me. I kept insisting that I knew Slokan Charles. He was my friend.

"He is?"

They all knew who he was, didn't they?

He was a leader of the international socialist movement, a foremost Marxist novelist and intellectual: the Third World's best.

Laughter.

I tried laughing too, making light of their combined levity and seriousness, their charges. More of the unrelenting heat; I was almost faint.

And I was glad finally to reach the Havana Libre. At once I asked for Dr Charles.

I was told he'd left, suddenly.

He had? He'd boarded a plane going out of Cuba that morning because he had a speaking engagement in Guyana. (*To my jailors I said I'd like to speak to someone from the Canadian Embassy. Please, one phone call.*)

I kept telling one accuser after another that I was involved in progressive activity in Canada; I was promoting socialist awareness, involved in peace and anti-nuclear activities. I planned starting a Canada-Cuba Friendship committee in Ottawa, which would spread to all the major cities in Canada.

More laughter.

Burt, the Calgarian, saw me in the hotel lobby looking pale, bedraggled. "You know, Slokan Charles was asking for you," he said. "He's had a longstanding ambition to become prime minsiter there." He was referring to Guyana: which was why Charles had gone back no doubt, all fired up because of the Conference rhetoric. Maybe he had met with Castro.

Now Charles, the fabulous raconteur, singing Cuba's praises to the poor of Guyana: a country now one of the poorest in the Third World, where people were hardly able to eke out a living. My father had written to me about this; though from time to time its leaders loudly expressed solidarity with the nonaligned countries of the Third World and championed the cause of the anti-apartheid struggle in South Africa.

Yes, Slokan Charles himself was now declaiming in the Guyana House of Assembly, an honoured guest speaker as he was–stirring his audience to thunderous applause. More visions of Elysian fields, as he kept spellbinding them with poetic, but mainly purple, phrases. And next he was going around the country and speaking to large gatherings, quoting Shakespeare, Milton, even Whitman and Emerson, to audiences that were largely illiterate.

(APPLAUSE)

Propped against a chair, I listened to the comments made by speaker after speaker on the final day of the Conference, the Cuban Minister of Education, smiling, more relaxed now. I imagined Charles coming up to me, saying in his best colloquial manner: "*Boy, Mannie, where the blasted hell you been, eh? You miss de best part o' the occasion, cause you didn't hear Comrade Leader Castro himself speak! He showed up finally, and it was because I was here, see. You shoulda hear him talk about transformation, the shift in the balance of forces in the world. Instead you went gallivantin' round the streets of Havana! What for, eh? What kind o' stupidness got into yuh head? You t'ink people not free to roam about here; you been takin' in too much blasted American an' Canadian propaganda. Cuba's a real communist society. You're seeing the real thing now, how they bringin' about economic, social, educational and cultural change! And equality taking place here for all classes, all races. D'you think such a thing could happen in Canada or America?*" He laughed hard.

But this image of a vital Dr Charles, full of life, didn't last.

Why did I keep seeing him a forlorn, almost tragic figure jogging along, throwing one dead leg after another in a mid-Western American city street–I didn't know. And disillusioned he was too; and I didn't know why. Departing, I was in the plane hovering above Havana. I looked out of the window, seeing a bare spot of terrain, island. I figured at that moment I was also watching Slokan Charles jogging slowly in the sweltering haze of the tropical sun...covering the seven-kilometer long path along the seawalls–the same one the Americans built in 1928 after their occupation of Cuba.

# TO SPEAK OF LEOPARDS

(A Novella)

## 1

Bellamy was gifted with the natural modesty of the Canadian. Being a poet didn't make a difference, of course. At first he was reluctant to talk: something about Bellamy, his manner, the way his eyes gleamed from time to time; chin, beard appeared to move. He'd recently returned to Canada after his long years in South America, he finally said; he'd gone there to "find himself": didn't I know?

But he was closer to the truth when he said it was the poetic impulse, latent in him then, that drove him. Eyes gleaming again, he talked about the sixties: he wanted experience for its own sake, the Vietnam War and all (somehow he figured he'd be drafted, a Canadian as he was; and suddenly he didn't want to). Then South America gripped him. I recalled his being imbued with the idea of feeding the starving millions there, teaching them to raise rabbits: and maybe the entire Third World would follow his example. Every village, all the poor peasants would raise rabbits, since the latter multiplied faster than chickens. Neither Helga (my wife, then: we were divorced now for almost three years) nor I knew him as a poet when we first met him. Helga, of course, had taken to him immediately: his eyes, tall bearing, his distinctively patched jeans–the only pair he seemed to own...and a certain priestly quality about him–captivated her.

"Ah, I shouldn't be talking about myself," Bellamy muttered.

"Please, go on," I encouraged, intrigued, so different in a way he looked now. I'd completely forgotten about Bellamy...until I met him here at the Heavenflower Café, this place where the down-and-out artists, poets (who played at verse and vociferously called themselves geniuses) met. Bellamy came here often, he said; and I, for no reason at all, dropped in this time... when our eyes met and recognized each other at once. It'd been almost fifteen years since we'd last seen each other...and Bellamy remembered in detail that first meeting with my wife and me. We'd come to Canada, fresh from Denmark, and were living in a semi-wilderness area in Northern Ontario, experimenting with a new life-style.

He smiled, enlivening his haggard appearance. How was she? he wanted to know.

I shrugged, I didn't really know; not intimately. I only sporadically kept in touch with Helga.

He seemed pained, yet the gleam in his eyes again. Just then he looked more like a missionary: and, indeed, he surprised me by saying he'd been one for a while.

I didn't ask about the rabbit farms (though over the years an image of this flashed into my mind, rabbit farms all over South America). When I finally told Bellamy this, he confessed to having had this same vision: once he saw himself as a Pied Piper, with the rabbits (not rats) following him wherever he went. Yes–he did go to South America: not only because of Ché Guevara and all he'd read about him and about socialism; or of what he knew about José Marti (he'd picked up Spanish quite easily, considering it one of the world's most fluid languages), a philosophy major as he'd been at Simon Fraser University on the West Coast–he was one of the first students to graduate from there. During those student years, as he recalled, he dabbled in the arts, politics, student protests. One day at a sit-in he came upon the works of Marti from the girl sitting next to him, a smallish, dark creature, almost birdlike, from South America. Her aquiline nose fascinated him; her entire being was made beautiful by it, he felt.

Bellamy said he made love to Yolanda that first time they met as she whispered to him about Marti. She'd also told him about the poet Nicolás Guillén, and sang to him from Neruda's *Captain's Verses*, which he was able to recite by heart later. And he'd wanted all his friends and colleagues on campus to do the same, to recite *The Captain's Verses* day and night, so fascinated, even obsessed, he'd become by it. He continued reading philosophy, being stimulated by Hegel, then Spinoza (Bellamy was part-Jewish, though he hardly ever admitted this to anyone). But–essentially–something about the father of the Cuban nation's raw energy, Marti's gusto, puritanism, his extolling the virtues of work: enthralled Bellamy. And one morning when he awoke, the idea of building things, layer upon layer, flashed into his mind: it stemmed from his internalized sense of the immense value of work for its own sake.

Yes, he'd started thinking about the ancient Egyptians building pyramids, the Mayans erecting monuments in Central America. Other pyramidal structures loomed up everywhere in his mind's eye all over Canada: the biggest on Parliament Hill in Ottawa. It almost frightened him the way his mind worked; it was then that he had an inkling of something extraordinary in himself.

To Helga and I after supper when we'd invited him home with us (on the outskirts of Thunder Bay, where American draft dodgers went to find themselves), he talked about the Third World with passion. And we–indeed new to the country–waxed warm to this unique American-Canadian (as we saw him).

Now we almost whispered to each other at the Heavenflower Café: talking, looking around at the poets. But ours was now the real poetry. Suddenly he lifted his head, said he was being watched. By whom?

"You must forgive me for being like this, my friend," he said. "But I've been under the shadow of men with guns."

Oh?

"Yes. I've been running from such men. Ah, you must understand what I'm trying to tell you, please." He grasped my arm, looked earnestly into my face. I knew at once: he was thinking of Yolanda again, his eyes suddenly luminous. Yolanda, you see, had told him he should go to Bolivia where some of the poorest in South America lived. "I had to go there," he muttered, looking around again. "Her parents were still there, you see, all members of the middle class. Her father a dentist, and nearly all his patients were Indians and mestizos." His eyes gleamed...on and off now, like the periodic switching on of small light bulbs.

"Ah, I lived among those Indians for awhile. That was what her father suggested. I sensed right away that he didn't like me. He felt Yolanda shouldn't have gone out with a bum like me. Yes, he called me that..a *BUM*! It was the only English word he knew well. I tried telling him Yolanda and I were friends, that was all." Bellamy's face twisted, mouth appearing lopsided. "He really did, believe me. Her father bribed the local postmaster and was able to censor my letters, having them all ripped up, all those who were writing to me from the West Coast, California. Yolanda, of course, told me these things much later. She confessed to not knowing her father really well; he always wanted to think of her as his pretty baby, that was all.

"Then one day he confessed to her that she was his bastard child. From then on she was bent on punishing him, which was why after university, she worked as a stripper in a nightclub in L.A.'' His mouth tightened. ''But Yolanda was also a Marxist. What she did with her body didn't matter. It was the cause that was most important.'' He looked forcefully at me, he'd agreed with her decision.

Then he shook his head, No, no; he didn't always understand her. What was really important were the questions she asked, her concern for the real people, the issues.

''Yolanda later ended up marrying a Democratic senator. We continued to write to each other mind you; she hadn't given up on me. You must understand, our relationship was like that.'' He looked around once more, then straight at me, eyes almost incandescent.

''What about the Indians?'' I asked.

He nodded. ''You see, the region was mountainous. One day the Indians took me to where the guerillas lived; and I was hoping to see the real revolutionary leader, Gonzalo Bragas, whom I'd heard being talked about a lot.'' Bellamy added it was then that he'd started putting words down on paper, writing a memoir. He was? He hoped to interview this Bragas, and one day even sell the interview to a prestigious paper such as *Le Monde* or *The Village Voice*, if he could get them interested in Bragas. He figured Bragas might even eventually become a popular leader, a powerful president: someone with the fame and stature of a Simon Bolivar.

But he wasn't able to see Bragas--he figured maybe they mistook him for someone working for the CIA.

Bellamy looked pained again.

Then he said that the poor Indians started looking up to him as a leader: their hero, a kind of god too maybe. It was incredible. Again he shook his head, looking a little embarrassed. ''It wasn't in my mould, you see. I only wanted to help them to help themselves, with rabbit farms everywhere. But I was certainly not a god...or a revolutionary of any sort. Deep down I was plain Jim Bellamy. Yes, I merely quoted Marti, that was all, idealistic as I was. And so were you, Sven, no?''

His calling my name sounded odd to my ears, because with the exception of Helga no one ever called me that (I remember--one night, Helga when she reached her orgasm, the one and only time throughout our marriage, she'd called out ''Sven, Sven,'' like a song). To everyone else, I was known as Steve, my Canadian name. ''I had to leave them, leave that village,'' Bellamy continued. ''I went to work in the silver mines, to experience true labour, you see; the dignity of it. Marti in me, no doubt: 'All men are good save who do not work.' Remember? Besides, how well can one truly know the suffering of the exploited if you didn't experience what they felt yourself?''

Experience was all, he insisted, lifting his head up; looking around again. "The Indians laboured in the silver mines; and I ate, slept next to them, exploited as they were–we all were." He spat out the word *exploited*. Yes, he stayed on for a whole year in the Casa de la Mancha silver mine.

Bellamy looked a little yellow, a sick yellow, and was it because of what he was telling me now?

Then he couldn't stand the exploitation any longer; he joined a group of fringe guerillas who called themselves *Zapatos*: a few members of this group seemed to have had training in Cuba. Some were also in the drug business, which of course he didn't know then. "You see, the Americans were giving arms to the military dictators everywhere in Latin America; their national security came first; not the poor Indians, these exploited people." Bellamy raised his voice, he'd become emotional.

"But there were many factions of guerillas, there was much fighting; and these *Zapatos*, by sheer force, wanted to bring them all together under one leadership. They hoped to do this by having lots of cash selling drugs. They had no qualms about working class black kids in the streets of America suffering because of what they were exporting. Those *Zapatos*," he added, "when I really got to know them--you see--were really kids themselves. Thirteen, fourteen-year-olds. I was alarmed. And their sisters and mothers were with them; ah, they had many groups you see." His mouth twisted, like a corkscrew; and once more he looked around.

"You, see, Sven," he continued, "one of the these same young people, a leader--as he called himself–I was alarmed by it...yes, he called me–not Bellamy–but Bethune. Yes, BETHUNE! I had risen from the grave in China now to be here among them. They were convinced of it."

"But Bethune was long dead," I said, alarmed.

He added that the *Zapatos* had read about Bethune, about Mao Tse Tung and his struggles in faraway China during the days of the revolution; and that from this experience they learnt that poor people could really transform their lives. All you need was the will-power. Yes...someone like....me...Bethune, their savior. "I'd read the American Edgar Snow's books about Mao," he added. "Yolanda had lent them to me (she'd stolen them from the university library). Oh, yes, the Indians insisted I was Bethune; even the young girls were calling me that, they with their warm, beautiful smiles. They were devoted Catholics too; to them I was truly Bellamy-Bethune."

More people kept entering the Café; but we seemed to be in a world all by ourselves.

I noticed one youth twitching his neck, then lifting his head, as if he'd swallowed cork and wasn't sure how to free himself of it.

Bellamy continued on, clutching my fingers. "How I wished Yolanda to see me then," he cried. "But she'd married the senator. Just prior to that she'd been a nude dancer in a club in the Bronx, she enjoyed watching the men's faces.

"Yolanda told me the filthy things she did on stage, putting a lighted cigarette on her pussy. What for? I asked her. She just laughed. Yolanda was really like that: daring. She dared everyone. She said the senator used to laugh at her antics, she'd given him so many kicks. I wondered why her father didn't censor that letter. At nights I'd reread all she wrote...all those details. Once or twice I cried."

Then, Bellamy admitted, he started believing himself to be Bethune.

"I started administering first aid; those skills came naturally to me. I saw bodies being ripped open by the military, many of these same young people ambushed, wounded, some killed brutally.

"Oh God, it sickened me. But what could I do? Me, Bethune-Bellamy, what did it matter what I called myself, what they called me? I was among the dead, the dying." He gesticulated, his entire body talking, veins talking, eyes, hands.

Then slowly he said: "You see, Sven, I realized there was a price on my head. Yes, the militarists wanted to get rid of me. I saw the posters myself, they were offering rewards, for me to be captived–dead or alive!"

A few heads turned, looking at us: because Bellamy's voice had risen a little. He sucked in air hard, studying me for awhile. Maybe he was also thinking about Helga, maybe wondering if she'd remarried.

I knew Helga was having an on-again, off-again relationship; but she was free now, she'd emphasized on the phone from Toronto when last we talked almost a year ago.

"I became a missionary soon after," Bellamy added. "It was the only thing I could do or become, seeking refuge in that flock." He made the sign of the cross, as if he forgot where he was; then said, "They were determined to capture me; it was the only way, and you know how the South Americans take to their priests, so religious they are. If I was to be arrrested, it'd be as a priest, carrying Christ's message to the flock. Yes–they found me. And they tortured me. I told them I was a Canadian. They said that Canadian or not, priests were revolutionaries, I'd be shot! I was marched off to prison, with a bunch of those same *Zapatos*, those kids, hollering for them to not take me away. One even called me Christ. Some of the women wept." Bellamy's eyes were like embers, an incandescent glow.

In prison, he wrote dozens of letters to Yolanda; all he could do, think about, were letters to her. He'd also written one to the President of Simon Fraser University.

"But, you know," said Bellamy, "her father was there, he seemed to be everywhere now. He had circulated a picture of me, one he'd found in Yolanda's letters kept at home. I was known everywhere in South and Central America. Brazil, Venezuela, Panama, El Salvador, Belize, even the Caribbean islands: they had that same picture of me."

He paused, and heaved. "The assholes at Simon Fraser thought nothing of me." He reflected hard. "Yolanda's senator husband was able to get the CIA to track down where I was, what prison I was held in," he growled. "They also contacted Interpol. They learnt that I was a convicted criminal, a thief and drug smuggler: it was a North American who was corrupting the simple and poor people of South and Central America. They wanted to stop it!

"And you see...Yolanda, well...she believed them. Her rabbit farmer-turned-dope peddler. Then one day she phoned, she'd gotten through to the prison where I was, and she wanted to come and visit me from New York, Queens, where she was living in a palatial home with her husband. She declared she was still in love with me. One night she woke up, perspiring, thinking about me. I asked her what about the Senator. She brushed this aside. She was desperately in love with me: in jail, about to be shot." He smiled, a little sadly. "I believed her, Sven."

"You did?"

He fidgeted, seemed nervous, eyes dilating. Then he shifted gear, talking about Canada: wondering if it was really a safe place for one like himself. He made allusions to the War Measures Act (indelible in my memory, because it was around that time Helga and I came to Canada). He also wanted to know if Canada really supported the South American military dictatorships, because Canada was so close to the American Administration. I told him I didn't know; I merely said Canada no longer faced a threat from the FLQ: though separatism was alive; maybe, Quebec one day would be a separate nation.

He nodded, he understood.

I asked, "Were there books that you read? Things you could do to while away the time, before they wanted to...shoot you?"

He grinned, as if I'd just asked a very naive question (how little I knew about South America). Ah, how I wanted Helga to be here with me now. Helga, who–while we were married–had an affair with a lumberjack in Thunder Bay–the best tree-climber in the region: a tall man, with ropes of muscles on his arms, thighs; somehow he'd *captivated* her as she'd said when I found out about their affair; and she'd threatened to leave me if I didn't forgive her. I had no choice.

"All the reading material, Sven, was about Devil's Island, you see. Papillon, his stuff." He looked at me hard, adding, "I read all that was there to read: all about Papillon's attempts at escaping, as if the militarists wanted to torture me further: this was the way they knew best, especially to us the Americans–they called me one. Ah, I began to realize what a man Papillon was, what inner resources he had, mad as he perhaps finally became. I imagined escaping, day after day. I prayed, nightly–I became a fervent believer in God. And I cursed my rabbit-farming ideals.

"Yes, I even thought about you and your marvellous wife Helga; such a lucky man you were. I also remembered the supper you cooked for me, she cooked for me."

I was flattered, and told him so. And yes–he fantasized making love to Helga a thousand times. Even when he was with Yolanda in his fantasies, he thought about Helga, and loved her (now he apologized for it).

A sudden but odd fury seized me, because he was able to make me see clearly Helga's beauty, which I'd taken for granted.

When I told Bellamy this, he advised that I write to her at once and ask her for forgiveness, even propose to her once more; though I knew Helga was really searching for the lumberjack (she figured he'd be in Toronto), eager to rekindle her powerful moments of passion with him. Then I figured that if I wrote to her to ask for forgiveness she'd despise me.

But Bellamy thought I was a fool. He said that if I did plead to Helga, I'd be gaining a beautiful woman in my life. The compensations of pleasure would be enough for the knocks on my psyche, my hurt pride. I reflected on this and looked at the phone for a long while; but was unable to bring myself to dial Helga's number.

## 2

In prison Bellamy began writing verse, the words coming easily to him, surprising him. And he talked about the creative process–he looked around to see if he had an audience–because, he said, faith had a hand in it, the creative process being an act of God no less. He affirmed that his gift would never have come to him if he hadn't been in jail waiting execution. Similar to what Dostoesvsky experienced, no?

His poems (when he showed them to me) were spare, intense. One was called "The Fetid Moon," and another "The Underground": these two only he wanted me to see first, the images of poverty and angst in them, as he recited in a slow voice.

I told him no North American publisher would touch these poems, because of their starkness; they were too melodramatic for the taste of readers of this continent.

He lowered his head, pulled at his face, pinching skin, as if reassuring himself that he was still here: maybe he'd become numb all over. No doubt Yolanda was still with him–tempered by Helga.

Now in a whisper he talked about aesthetic theory, which he'd muttered to the half-drunk jailor at his prison door. One day the latter asked him to recite the Bible to him, if he was indeed a priest and a poet; Hidalgo only wanted him to recite in *inglés*, though he knew little of the language (he wanted all his life to learn English). Bellamy's eyes lit up; yes, he was was able to recite parts of the New Testament to his jailor, and how could this have come to him if it wasn't a miracle?

Soon after Hidalgo was converted, and he wanted to help Bellamy escape; it wasn't right for a priest to be locked up like this, Hidalgo said. Yes, he'd take Bellamy to a lion-tamer in a circus, someone reliable. Hidalgo made the sign of the cross.

Bellamy paused.

Suddenly I was thinking of the numerous animal references in his poems: his knowledge of South American animals amazing me. The condor, mountain hawks, llama, wolf.

"I got out by the skin of my teeth, you might say," Bellamy muttered. "Yes, I pretended I was a hyena, a beast of many forms, then the jaguar, this most indigenous of South American animals. Ah, you see, the jailor loved my animal stories. I told them they all came from the Book of Revelation.

"You see, Sven, South Americans love stories about the jaguar; a jaguar chasing a crescent moon... how they love that one. Then Hidalgo said I reminded him of his wife, because she was really old-style Spanish. Gloomy, tragic." Bellamy managed a smile.

"Hidalgo was also fat, very fat, yet always toting a gun," he added. "He loved life more than he loved death, he said." Again Bellamy smiled. "You see Sven, I began telling him that all these animals were from the Garden of Eden. He came towards me in the cell. You see, he was a homosexual, as I'd suspected. Believe me, I had to give myself to him; all my talk seemed nothing at that moment. But I wanted to be free, maybe I was going a little mad. The jailor kept repeating the names of all the animals. Yes–after that first experience, sweating...and in pain...I wrote my first poem."

Bellamy revealed that only then, in distant and dark South America–the truth of Freud's insights came to him...and something about real angst as well...what it meant to truly suffer...and sex...all came to him in a moment of blinding truth.

Then Bellamy confessed to making love with Hidalgo seven times. "Seven is a magical number; after, it had to stop. By then we started despising each other. Hidalgo said he was having twinges of guilt, he began fearing for his soul in hell, and Baby-Jesus flying about him with wings flapping noisily. He'd wake up at nights sweating, while his morose wife wiped beads of perspiration from his face, neck, arms. The next day he quickly set about arranging for me to escape. Which I did."

Bellamy added with a labouring breath that it wasn't easy to get out of the country. Suddenly Hidalgo wanted him back in the prison; he'd snitched on him.

Bellamy paused...as if not sure what to say next.

Then he revealed that he was discovered by a young girl in a barn, just when the police were about to pounce on him. She at once reminded him of Yolanda. (Why did he dream one night that Yolanda had died from an overdose of pills?) He muttered, "My ideals were all dying...one by one..all those rabbits I kept seeing going up to heaven in an odd dream were now going away from me. And I wanted to go with them, but they kept leaving me behind, their white fluffiness swirling, floating away. And this girl, so young, Rosa was her name; a circus girl really. Yes, I saw the gypsy in her at once. Her father, she said, was in charge; they'd go to the villages close to the mountains and perform. She'd persuade her father to take me on.

"I did everything, watering the horse, currying them, feeding the goats that talked like old men, taking care of mice that wore pince-nez. Then, after the lion-tamer one morning died suddenly of a strange illness, I was asked to take his place."

Bellamy looked around, nervous, and I expected something harrowing to come from his lips. I also imagined the soldiers searching for him everywhere, and not in the least expecting that this priest-cum-lion tamer still to be in the country.

He smiled. "I began enjoying what I was doing, working with the animals. Being a lion-tamer involved risks. Maybe Hidalgo really had this planned. Maybe he figured I had a knack with animals."

He closed his eyes, thinking about Hidalgo: reciting to him. Quietly.

He whispered, "You see, animals are not worse than human beings."

Next he said that his particular interest shifted from the jaguar to the leopard. It wasn't a lion-tamer that he was, but a tamer of leopards; one creature in particular. He liked looking at the creature's eyes; the way it growled. "You sense that you are constantly in some primeval forest." He held his breath, awe written all over his face.

"I knew the military police wouldn't look for me here. Maybe they'd come to laugh at the circus. Not to ferret me out. I spent long hours with this one leopard with split earlobes, even talking to it at times. I began to feel I had a special bond with it.

"One night I fell asleep, and I'd left the leopard's cage open. And, you see–Rosa came out of her tent, saw me, and she thought at any moment the leopard would dash out of the cage, the maneater as it was--as she called it. And tear me to pieces. No?

"She'd grown really fond of me. She was Yolanda all over, though she had a funny way of laughing. She told me that the previous animal-trainer had a bad temper,and the animals knew it; he always carried a whip and gun. She was very impressed with my ease, my style...no fear in me. Her father was also very impressed. Yes, that leopard–maneater--with luminous eyes, spotted yellow and black coat. It struck terror in the hearts of everyone. When the circus was on show, women and children screamed as they saw it. It was the ultimate terror."

Bellamy looked intensely at me; as if, suddenly, the maneater was with us here in the Café.

A chill went down my spine.

And it was as if Bellamy was the leopard, silent, dark, ready to snarl; he, close to me...and I was his captive.

"You know, it's so good to see you again," he said.

And laughed.

I looked around, looking at the faces in the Café. I turned to Bellamy again. I asked, "What about the leopard? Tell me more."

He breathed in hard, his entire rib cage rising. "Ah, you want to know. Maybe you're a little like the South Americans too, no?"

I figured Bellamy needed an audience; as an animal-trainer it was what he craved most. It wasn't raising rabbits to feed the starving milions of South America that he wanted, but being with the circus...that animal!

"It was dark, and the leopard came out and was licking my face. You see, like a weird dream, I was so close to death, I felt; maybe I dreamt I was dying,and all the time the leopard kept licking my face."

He closed his eyes. "Rosa, you see, was petrified: and she heard a sniffing, heavy breathing sound; as if the leopard was talking to me. But she screamed. Oh God, this really frightened the animal, and it bounced back into the cage. Then Rosa rushed close to me, her own life in danger. She held me in her arms. She really did–the first time. And maybe they should get rid of the leopard, kill it! They must! And she kept caressing, asking me if I was okay, shaking all over; while the leopard growled, going around and around in its cage. It was strange, a miracle. She was kissing me all over, and praising God."

I figured Bellamy enjoyed telling me this; and he paused... I waited expectantly. "Go on, please." It was the first time I showed so much eagerness.

"Her father, Manuel, came out to see what all the commotion was about. He saw Rosa kissing me fervently, and he was mad. He accused me of sleeping with her...his WIFE! Yes, Rosa all along was his wife, didn't I know that?

"I shook my head. Rosa was in tears, poor girl...woman. Manuel, he threatened to kill me, to use a machete to chop my head off! No, he'd get a gun. It was the end of my life. No more circus for me. *No mas*!

"But Rosa, crying, said it wasn't so at all. That it was a miracle I'd been saved. Yes, a true miracle! The leopard,she said, didn't kill me because I was special. She was really incoherent now. She kept telling him how the leopard had come out and was patting me with its paws...something really incredible."

Bellamy looked around before continuing:

"You see, that Manuel, so little did I know–he made the sign of the cross, and what a religious man he was all his life. Yes, it was indeed a miracle, right here...during his life time...he'd never heard of a thing like this, especially when I was so defenceless."

He smiled a little.

"Ah, *amigo*," Bellamy called me that now, so carried away he was. "That Rosa and Manuel became my closest friends: especially Manuel. Yes, he told me that they'd been trying a long time to have a child, but couldn't. And maybe,now, what I had experienced, would bring them good luck."

He laughed.

"God was close to them, said Manuel. And yes, he knew I'd been a priest, but in jail: and he knew I was wanted everywhere by the *policia*. He made the sign of the cross once more."

I knew then that Bellamy didn't want to continue; he was stalling; as if there was something he preferred not to say. Something to do with Rosa.

He took out a cigarette and started smoking, he whom I didn't think smoked.

Please, you must go on, I was telling him.

But he remained quiet; looking around once in a while, though not in a paranoid fashion anymore.

Finally, not looking at me in the eye, he confessed to making love to Rosa. And maybe Manuel, her husband, knew and encouraged it. He wanted her to become pregnant, and that would be the "miracle" indeed!

He looked at me, breathing in hard. He added, "You see, even when I was making love to Rosa, she kept talking about my being so close to the leopard (she called it a panther, the maneater). She said the panther had once mauled a pregnant woman, many years ago.

"She became suddenly afraid. From then on, she began acting strangely. And we stopped making love for a while; she even thought me impotent, accused me of it. Now she told her husband in detail about how we'd made love each night." Bellamy closed his eyes, he seemed in another world all by himself.

"Manuel came to confront me while I was with the leopard, and he said, 'Ah, *señor*, you make it wid me *esposa*, no? You, saint, you make it wid her, ha. Maybe you really give her a child, eh?' He kept laughed, as if a strange madness had suddenly gripped him. Next he was pleading, saying, 'You work for me still, eh?'

"Next Rosa was beside him, her teeth chattering, her lips twitching, and I figured she'd become sick. She started vomiting.

"Manuel kept laughing uncontrollably, saying, 'Ah, *Señor* Bell-am-i, maybe you really give her a child now, eh? You did, eh? Ha, ha, ha!'"

## 3

I fantasized being Bellamy: being with him all over South America. This feeling overcame me, the latent desire to experience the untamed; to be totally uninhibted in all that I did, felt. It dawned on me that I'd been cut off from vital experiences all my life: unlike Bellamy. I began to feel too that Canada wasn't offering me what I wanted. Was Canada too much like Denmark? My deeper instincts hadn't been aroused; the world around me was too predictable, orderly. I yearned to rub my hands against a jaguar's or a leopard's coat, to hear such a creature snarl; to look long and hard into the iridiscence of its eyes and contemplate on the aesthetics therein. The world was suddenly topsy-turvy, my brain cells rattling like seeds in a pod. And, I figured, meeting Bellamy again was perhaps itself a miracle. And how I wished Helga to see him now. Then, no, I didn't want to share him with anyone.

Bellamy smiled, a little beatifically. Then he began talking about my reconciling with Helga; and perhaps he was the unifying force I was longing for. Then I remembered something that Helga and I had talked about around the time we were getting divorced: about our fate, karma; and maybe in a few years' time we'd perhaps make an effort to remarry. Then our lovemaking would be better; then, too, she might completely forget about her lumberjack beau, who I heard had become a born-again Christian and considered love-making a SIN! Ah, my fateless Helga...her faith-filled lover...now climbing a tree to knock on heaven's door!

And she'd be returning to my outstretched arms...only...our grand reconciliation. It was what Bellamy wanted, which I saw clearly in his eyes. The night now creeping up on us; the others in the Café laughing, boisterous, their own poetry shrieked out with heavy tongues, foul gestures, a bottle of aerated drink fizzing and spilled out at the end of a short poem, symbolism of climactic love. Next, the performance poets lunged anew with the senses, such posturing...one struggling to be free from the self, being Hinduist and Buddhist simultaneously. The haiku night grew deeper, anguished.

The Irish-Cuban owner of the Café, a fifty-five year old who insisted that he was a poet (though he'd never really published anything), someone whose family had flourished in Havana–he'd once been an impressario for Batista and had been married for the third time at the young age of twenty-three–but who fled Cuba once Castro came into power–now sat with us and listened; then he left us, only to return again. The others were slowly leaving now.

Bellamy began speaking about the essence of the soul's being, and how he'd taken to reading the Bhagavada Gita (a volume he'd picked up in a second-hand store, translated by Christopher Isherwood). Yes, he also recalled Krishnamurti's "let every leaf first be green"; only then, must one set about transforming the world, he asserted.

He looked deeply at me.

The owner of the Café returned again, said he must close shop, but he invited us to sit with him upstairs (where he lived) to continue our conversation. And in the scarce light of the upperroom, almost dark as it was–where Marco lived alone–we continued on.

Bellamy revealed that he'd really become an expert on leopards; and maybe one day he'd write a book for the National Geographic Corporation. Leopards, he reminded us (the Cuban deeply engrossed in him): *Panthera pardus*... at one time roamed over Great Britain; was found in Japan, Africa, India, and eastern Asia. Yes, Bellamy said he was one of the first people to make the distinction between a panther and a leopard, the former being a large leopard really, usually the male. He said he'd developed a special interest in black panthers. Because of his semi-radical days at Simon Fraser? he wondered.

Leopards aren't really spotted, and didn't seem to belong anywhere really, Bellamy added: but were indigenous to Abyssinia and the East Indies. He'd actually observed leopards snatching fish with their powerful jaws in narrow South American rivers. He'd also seen tree-climing leopards doubling as jaguars.

Bellamy had continued to travel all over South and Central America, with Rosa close to him; and he didn't worry any longer about the fascist *policia*. And Rosa, who'd recovered after losing her child, kept reminding him that the dictators were really fickle; they were like children–she knew because she was the daughter of one–they loved you one moment, then hated you the next. "Just like some animals, *Senor* Bell-a-mi," Rosa averred.

Then in Uruguay, the maneater lost both its teeth in a freak accident, to the utter dismay of Manuel and Rosa (the latter thought it might mean bad luck), Bellamy said.

"Latins," he muttered, leaning close to our faces (the Cuban bending foward), "have a great love relationship with panthers, more than with jaguars."

Then Bellamy said that in between his travels he'd read Borges and Marquez: he'd even met the latter, and spent an entire evening talking about Latin American fixation with animals, though after a while they simply discussed Octavia Paz's views on the subject.

He continued on about the circus (he kept switching back and forth), which had about thirty people, including all the "little people"; and next they went to the Caribbean. But the Blacks never appreciated jaguars or leopards: which was surprising. Now he told us that one night in Haiti while sleeping in the intense humidity, he dreamt he'd come face-to-face with Erzulie, the beautiful voodoo goddess, her lithe black figure naked before him, with a whip in hand (she who was reputed to be more beautiful than Nefertiti).

Marco breathed hard next to me, so engrossed he was.

Bellamy let out a short laugh.

"She, Erzulie, took me for a zombie, you see. Her sinewy hips wiggled before me,as she commanded me to make love to her. It was the only way I could prove to her that I was really alive. But I wanted to be faithful to Rosa: to tell Erzulie this, but the words didn't come out. Then too, I figured I'd completely lost my fear of Manuel, bad-tempered as he was."

Bellamy said he'd made love to Rosa again, and she cried in his arms; and he too cried. And Rosa said to him that she wanted to have children...a whole soccer field of them; all night she kept saying this while her husband snored heavily in the opposite tent. It was the first time she'd stayed the entire night with him.

Next he admitted that suddenly the circus wasn't the same anymore. In a small town (after they'd exhausted the Caribbean and all the voodooienne aspects they'd brought into their acts), they found themselves outside Mexico City, El Doloroso, noted for its figurine horses. It was here that the maneater disappeared! Stolen? No one knew. The entire town's *policía* went looking for the beast, but without luck.

Bellamy said he cried for a full two hours, so attached he'd become to the animal, which was really his mascot. And Manuel and Rosa cried bitterly also. And the Chief of Police (the shortest Bellamy had ever seen, just a little under five feet) also cried, since he felt that his town's reputation would now sufffer throughout the Americas.

Bellamy confessed that he'd never been the same again. Though that very night of their tremendous grief, Rosa whispered to him, "I am pregnant again, Señor Bell-a-mi."

"But the father, *el papa*, who is he?" he'd asked.

"Ah, *Señor, es me niño. Yo tengo niño ahora.*"

Bellamy said he wasn't sure if he was indeed the father, or someone else, since he'd found her caressing one of the "little people."

But Rosa was too excited now, which depressed Bellamy for an entire week; and he thought seriously of death–so deep was his depression.

All the while, Rosa only rejoiced. It was then, once more, that he'd begun to think of creativity, poetics, philosophy. About man's purpose in the world.

When she calmed down, Rosa said to him: "Ah, Señor, is it the panther why you're now sick?"

He looked at the joyful expression on her face; and right then–as if a shining realization suddenly came to him–he started making plans to return to Canada.

## 4

What about Yolanda? Had he completely given up on her? It seemed incredible...Rosa, for as long as he knew her, was perhaps just a passing phenomenon. But Yolanda–if not Helga–was his real love. A shadow, like a heavy pall, crossed his face. The oil lamp flickered in the Cuban's small livingroom.

Yolanda had been divorced from her senator husband: a settlement had been reached out of court, which left her with a small fortune. But money, Bellamy said, didn't mean much to her; she was only looking for love, happiness, as she'd confessed to him. Bellamy looked at the Cuban, then at me. The lamp flickered once more. Ah, yes, Yolanda had subsequently found what she was looking for in Mustapha Smith, a black jazz musician in Washington, D.C. Yolanda took to him because of the poignancy of his music: she'd cried when she first heard him play the horn. But when he made love to her, well, he was...a showoff! And after she'd begun living with him he told her he was a Vietnam vet, one-legged as he was, and he'd become a fanatical Muslim whose interest in Malcom X had never waned despite the passing of the years (Bellamy suddenly fished out a bundle of letters,all postmaked Washington, D.C. to prove that his correspondece with Yolanda was alive all these years).

Yes, Mustapha Smith got her interested in the Black Muslims by quoting whole passages from Malcolm X's writings, which Yolanda began intensely reading. Bellamy quoted from one of her letters..."*Love, humility, and true brotherhood was almost a physical feeling wherever I turned. All are One and slept as One. Everything about the pilgrimage atmosphere accentuated the Oneness of Man under One God.*" He repeated the words again, like an epiphany: it was for such gems that he kept her letters, to bolster him in his moments of depression and near-desperation.

And Yolanda confessed that there was something special about being so close to a man with one leg, the stump on his right hip fascinating her endlessly. *Believe in Allah, she heard over and over again from his lips; He is the one and true God, and follow the ways of his prophet Mohammed*!

Thereafter Bellamy plunged deeper into poetic theory and religio-philosophy. He'd begun seriously writing again, inspired by Yolanda's letters about her devotion and sincere love for Mustapha. He'd also begun travelling through the dark night of the soul; and how he wished he was still with the circus, imagining Rosa with her baby, breast-feeding her before the circus spectators who applauded; and would the baby end up being one of the "little people"?

He wrote to Yolanda again. But...his letter, two months later, returned with the words written large across the envelope "MOVED". Later, upon phoning her ex-husband, he learnt that Yolanda and Mustapha had taken off to Africa: that they were last heard to be in Gambia, where they hoped to find Mustapha's African roots. And maybe...hers as well, since he'd convinced her that the father of mankind was really in Africa.

And, said Bellamy, voice low—as if he was truly exhausted—that was how he ended up in Ottawa, because he'd come here to meet officials of the Department of External Affairs on Sussex Drive, whom he wanted to persuade to meet with those of the Gambian Embassy so they could track down Yolanda. He feared for her safety.

Yes, finally, they were able to contact her.

She replied to him saying she was flattered he'd tried to find her. She also told him she remembered his dream of starting rabbit farms all over the starving Third World, and she'd told Mustapha Smith about this, and he wanted to meet him...this *Canadian*! And maybe, he—Bellamy—might help them to get some money, because they were now completely broke. Yes, she wanted money, urgently; and he'd wasted no time in sending them all (very little) he had.

Recently Yolanda had wired him to send some more money.

Again he looked pained.

"Where's Yolanda now?" I asked.

The Cuban was also very intrigued. He looked at the dying lamp, and a strong wind was blowing outside; then he looked at Bellamy again, whose face seemed gaunt, chiselled close to the bone.

"Ah, yes, I've heard from Yolanda. She's living again in New York City, in Queens."

Close to her senator husband? I wondered.

"With Mustapha Smith?" the Cuban impulsively asked, as if he was willing to place a bet on it.

"No. They split up. Love being elusive, you understand," said Bellamy. "And Mustapha Smith was now Mustafa Maphalele, who had succumbed to drugs, and was still in Africa, maybe Burundi, making a living by showing off his stump and talking about the horrors of the Vietnam War to university students, five or ten at a time, who cared to listen and laugh. Then he was heard to be attracting nubile tribal women so he could sleep with them."

"What's she doing in Queens?" asked the Cuban, his Latin sympathies now fully alive.

"Ah," Bellamy said dully, looking away from both of us, "she's now in an ashram run by Swami Ram Babu-baba. She's been there for the last three months." He paused. "Maybe she's still there."

The way he said this, it sounded like a lost hope, or an illusion. Bellamy breathed in heavily. Wheezed.

"She wants nothing to do with the outside world, imbued as she is with Oneness, Wholeness; with Sanctity and Love, and Divinity."

Bellamy then took out a volume of verse he'd had printed himself on cheap paper, the brown cover really nondescript, dull. But in it were poems of a genuine spiritual fervour. And it seemed we were the first to see this collection, which also contained a semi-poetic discourse on aesthetic theory–unlike anything ever written before; which confounded all the textual and deconstructionist critics, even though he referred to Aristotle in it from time to time.

"You see," Bellamy affirmed, holding my hand in a fierce grip, "I began to become aware, with greater clarity, with Yolanda's letters next to me, that literature–all art–and spirituality were one. Myth in process is a marvellous thing, Sven. Really heightened spirituality."

I looked at the volume, noting that it was dedicated to Yolanda.

But a few of the poems were dedicated to Sheena, which was the name of the maneating leopard; and it was these poems that I began reading earnestly because of the clarity of vision and the passion in them. They were more powerful than anything Neruda or anyone had written. He started reciting a few lines, at the urging of the Cuban, and both of us began to feel then as if the universe was in the process of changing.

I closed my eyes in the silence of the night. With Bellamy, I felt, I was being tranfigured. He said in the end, like a further truth–when all truths were now suddenly one: "Yolanda will come back to Canada one day, to be with me. It's like Helga coming back to you, Sven." He looked luminously at me. "Adorable woman, that Helga, just like Yolanda, maybe. And at that time, there will be absolute Oneness. For now, though, we have to suffer by being alone, what is also a form of art." He continued on like this, but I no longer keenly listened to him; though the Cuban was.

For I was thinking of Helga more passionately than ever. Longing for her, intensely. And I knew her phone number, where she lived in Toronto.

I decided to call her now.

While the Cuban still listened to Bellamy, I dialled the number in an adjoining room. Rehearsing in my mind all that I'd say to her...and praying that someone would answer the phone.

A man without an accent answered. He said his name was Forrestal. The lumberjack? The blood grew cold in my veins.

He said it was one o'clock in the morning, and why did I call so late? Yes, Helga was there...but who was I? He was becoming agitated. No, she wasn't alseep; they were awake all the while. Helga grabbed the phone from him, I could sense. Right away I began telling her:

"I've met Bellamy today; I have, Helga. D'you remember him? You must!"

I continued excitedly, hardly giving her a chance to reply. "Bellamy, whom you adored; whom you talked about so much. Remember, Helga?" Oh, how I wanted her to remember him. "He's real, alive with me here tonight. He still adores you!"

She said she couldn't remember him. She didn't know who I was talking about.

"Who's he anyway?"

"Who is he?" I almost shouted into the phone, unable to control myself.

I thought I heard this Forrestal trying to take the phone away from her, and mumbling in the background to hang up on me. She and her lumberjack beau: they'd found each other again no doubt. And then she began telling me, calling me Steve (not Sven), that she intended going back to Denmark; maybe for good; and she was taking Forestall with her; and maybe they'd get married there.

It was the end of the world for me; I was lost in Canada. Slowly I put the phone down; even as Helga was still calling out to me, asking me not to be depressed: that she hadn't forgotten me, that she meant to tell me this a long time ago. Yes, she was much in love; and she was tired living alone. Nature abhorred a vacuum, didn't I know? Damn it! And only in Denmark could she... find that oneness of being; not here in Toronto, in Canada!

It was to Bellamy that I turned. But he was no longer there.

The Cuban looked at me, blinking; the lamp now almost without light. He shrugged, and smiled. Both of us thinking of other realities.

Further spaces.

And, finally, translucent moments of unimaginable bliss.

# DONATO

The Canadians were giving the first electric train to Manazama, which wasn't too far from the high Andes: a place that was obscure and simultaneously out of reach, it appeared; where all was often quiet save for the occasional rumbling, distinct and indistinct noises. Yet in three hours by car I arrived there from the capital, Lima. The "presentation" of the train was an event I didn't want to miss, because–finally–I'd see Señor Donato. He was a legend before I was born, I heard from the Indians; and, I pictured him an old man, short, paunchy: a figure not unlike Napoleon's perhaps with a short jutting-out neck and looking like a deformed crow; but a man very distinctive nevertheless, his sharp eyes constantly peering into you I was told.

I'd heard also that Donato was a Canadian, which was why he'd be there at the presentation. I thought this incredible, the more I dwelled on it, my eagerness increasing the closer I got there. The train, of course, was the first of its kind to be used in South America: the *Helmsmith 4200* being a unique product; it could eat up terrain that meandered in a maze-like, circuitous fashion, built especially for mountainous territory such as the Andes. The research I'd done indicated Donato was from English parentage, with a strong dose of Italian. I'd learnt also that he had a touch of North American Indian and French in him: a man who seemed to have every nationality in him the more I enquired about him.

My writer's instinct (I was a travel journalist who'd been casually tipped off about Donato from a contact in the Department of External

Affairs in Ottawa) led me to enquire further about Donato, to ferret out his story, intrigued as I was about him. From some of the Indians I'd learnt that he was almost like a god to them, even as they laughed when they discussed, talked, about him. They unquestionably—perhaps simply—loved him!

Oddly, when I set eyes on him, Donato didn't look that old; definitely not a man struggling to uphold an autocratic or supercilious bearing. A black patch on one eye, he looked unique, even intimidating. He limped a little, his left leg throbbing, as if with spasms, which no one had told me about (some sort of deformity no doubt). He was in his sixties, but still vibrant—with a beautiful, tall, dark Spanish-looking woman, who was solemn, constantly by his side. Donato smoked a mauvish pipe, as he watched the official speaker representing the Province of Manazama wind down his speech. Then the ribbon was cut and everyone, about fifty people altogether, raised their glasses to toast the new train.

Then another garrulous city official, the Mayor no doubt, the tallest and thinnest man I'd seen in these parts with extremely long jet-black whiskers, lavishly thanked the Canadian government, his tone unctuous, even fawning. How was Donato taking it all? He merely kept smoking,a little compulsively, though suavely. When I finally sidled up to him, he said he'd heard someone like me would show up. Did he mean my profession? He listened carefully to the tall Mayor Hernandez, and laughed. Looking directly at me next, he murmured: "This train, it's fascinating for Manazama." The manner in which he said this appeared as if he didn't approve, a distinct flash in his eyes as he scowled and looked away, concentrating on Hernandez again.

"Fascinating?" I asked quietly, bringing him back to me.

He sucked at his pipe, which was slightly gilded at the sides. I was now in the habit of smoking one myself, though I'd tried hard to kick the habit almost two years ago.

Donato inhaled smoke, and the pipe looked absolutely perfect on him. With a delicate, assured air he pulled his glass to his lips, swallowing his drink like a strange bird. Sadie, his female companion, unobtrusively slipped away to join another group (maybe it was because of my presence, the one expected); and, maybe, Donato was really looking forward to talking to me alone, I figured—smoke swirling in tendrils in the South American air. An arabesque of doubt, vague shadow: no, I wasn't mistaken.

"You been here long?" he asked, quickly.

"Long enough to know all about you," I said.

He smiled.

Later I learnt that Donato had a habit of doing this to people, making them feel uncomfortable (as he did me now).

"What part of Canada are you from?"

"Montreal."

"Ah." He sipped his champagne again, eyes lighting up, but another moment he concentrated on the crowd, the officials, their wives, daughters, who were suddenly talkative, chippy: as if this was really the festive event no one ever wanted to miss. Donato was assessing each one: and I looked around, hardly seeing an Indian about, they who'd be using the train. I wanted to ask him about this, but a group of people converged on Donato, and words swirled about him, a clatter, jabber of phrases, gushes of endless laughter, half-jibes, mocking in tone.

"Ah, Señor Donato, it's so nice to see you! So really wonderful!" the words came: men and women fawning about him; and Sadie, again close by, smiled, almost as if she'd orchestrated this–to get him away from me.

"Ah, how well you look, Señor Donato. You're truly marvellous to be here; to share this event with us," said another in a haughty voice.

Donato indulgently smiled, though unshaken by the flattery, the fatuous words: he knitted his eyebrows and nodded politely. Someone else–one of the official ladies–added loudly: "The Canadians, you see, are splendid people; they're so inventive. We could do with some of that kind of inventiveness here in Manazama, no?" She wore a peacock-blue hairstyle, her voice unexpectedly highpitched as someone just then referred to her as Doña Pizarro. All eyes turned to me for a moment, the perhaps conspicuous other Canadian.

"Yes, indeed," someone else said, a man with huge dark eyes that seemed to contain the entire Andes. "Maybe the Americans will follow the Canadians," he added, like a rebuke; and Dona Pizarro grimaced and stopped midway of a further remark.

Then Donato, too solemnly, said: "Manazama also has its inventive people." His words seemed forced out of him, putting an end to their flutter, excitement.

Sadie came forward, her cologne saturating the air, and whispered, "He wishes you to dine with him."

I was immensely pleased. I figured now I'd get to know him better. I didn't know where he actually lived, though it was assumed he lived, vaguely, somewhere in the mountains. Then Sadie walked off, distant again.

In Donato's limousine, sleek-looking and jet-black, like a hearse--we hardly talked. Sadie also seemed commanded to silence. Donato muttered, "How do you like it here?" He spoke a slow, heavily accented English, emphasizing every syllable. It was difficult to tell that he was a Canadian now.

"It's very scenic," I said.

Donato looked outside, as if taking in the view for the first time. He didn't say anything more.

Sadie suddenly said, "You must tell me why you think it *iss* scenic, Señor." Donato sucked at his pipe, looking back once or twice and then oddly leaning forward a little, almost as if he was expecting us to be followed.

I shifted my attention back to Sadie, who now began to be quite friendly. I'd heard she was absolutely devoted to Donato: that he'd taken care of her since she was a child. When I spoke again, she laughed, unconvinced by what I said.

She had another question for me, this time about Canadian politics: which seemed staid to her, all that I now said about federalism, though she listened as if intrigued. "*Iss* it true the French in Montreal want to separate from the rest?" she asked.

Donato leant forward a litte, perhaps eager to hear my answer.

* * *

We arrived at a palatial-looking concrete structure, a large tract of land surrounding the house. He was a landlord of some sort: or how else did he live? It suddenly dawned on me Donato had one of the biggest land holdings in all of Manazama, a region bigger than half the size of England. "I've been here for almost a quarter of a century, Richard," he said, calling me by my first name.

"That long?"

The distinct black patch of one eye peered into me. "The Indians, you see, they want me here," he said. "They need me." In the conviction of what he said, something also irked. He added, "I belong here with them. They're like my children–so they seem to think."

"But–" I attempted.

"You will understand. I am their father maybe, some think. But there's the embarrassment of it you see." He sucked in air, then added: "But I don't really care for that.You know, very soon they'll be a revolution here. The peasants, they're awakening everywhere in Latin America. What good will that do, eh?"

Yes, rumblings of uprisings: I'd been hearing them all the time; one recently in a faraway district called Cuchito. But no one talked openly about this; everyone seemed held to a strange silence.

Donato laughed a little heartily, his face ruddy, ears wiggling. "You understand what I am saying? I want you to write about this, *mon ami*." He eyed me sharply, and at once I realized why Donato had invited me here.

"That train"–he added a little later over dinner consisting of roast duck and cassava dumpling–"will soon be in the hands of those struggling for freedom." He paused. Then: "Maybe the Canadians have made a mistake."

I remained quiet.

"The *Helmsmith 4000*, it's a good model. Excellent I should say. It was manufactured in Montreal you know." He went on to elaborate, all about the technicalities of this train, and I began taking notes.

Sadie smiled as she watched me; maybe she was more amused at the way I was taking in Donato. The servants came around with other dishes, and they seemed happy, smiling: his *niños*.

"The guerrillas will need a lot of technical expertise to be able to use it," I ventured.

"Guerrillas?" He stopped eating.

I nodded.

"No, they're not guerrillas, Richard. Maybe, if things fall into the wrong hands, perhaps then they will become guerrillas. But not now." Cryptic; a strange light in his eyes.

Slowly, Donato began to reveal something else, which in retrospect–up to this day–I still found shocking: Donato, you see, was the leader of a band of peasants; all his bourgeois trappings were really a front; and the peasants, these proletariat (or guerrillas) accepted him for what he was.

I looked at Sadie–she, one of his lieutenants no doubt–well trained in using a variety of weapons and in guerilla tactics (I now learnt that she was also a trained doctor). I figured she knew the peasants' way of life very well, was adept in their many dialects, customs.

Donato got up and took me to a special room in the cellar where he had an assortment of weapons–and wines–which he said was regularly shipped out to the peasants fighting across the Andean plains. He also told me he'd met acquaintances of Zapata, and he talked about them: old men with their teeth gone, who were children when they rallied on Zapata's side; they–who remembered everything on warm nights under a distant moon and stars.

Wasn't he afraid I was going to reveal this to the rest of the world? Maybe...something in me convinced him I wouldn't. I knew the military leader of the province, General Zaf, who'd be glad to get his hands on this information. "I'm still a Canadian," Donato added, looking at me. " A bit like extra-territoriality perhaps, my being here, I mean." He smiled.

"But you'd be overthrowing the government of this country. You could be shot," I ventured.

He scoffed. "One day, perhaps. But not now." His eyes hardened, like snooker balls.

We talked late into the night, Donato doing most of it. Then it was time for me to return to my hotel. Donato said he'd much prefer if I stayed at his palace.

But I declined; this was expected of me.

"You will be driven back to town," he said. "But come tomorrow, there's more to talk about. "

On the way to my hotel, my thoughts whirling, I knew I wouldn't be able to sleep well that night. Torturous dreams, akin to nightmares perhaps; Donato had mentally tired me out; and Sadie, smiling.

* * *

The next day Donato too busy to speak to me. Sadie also seemed very busy, even though she sat with me for a few minutes at a time.

"What's going on?" I asked her.

"There's been an attack."

"An attack?"

"Yes. Maybe it's just a rumour."

"Rumour?" I asked inanely.

"It's been known to happen before. But we can't take chances. Lives are at stake." She was tense.

Now everything seemed confusing; after all, Donato was in the middle of bringing about substantial changes in the country. And maybe his elegance, style, as well as his dourness, were all part of the front he cultivated. And from the peasants I'd learnt that the electric train came about as a result of his doing. That very train would be part of the symbol of the transformation, the revolution. I wanted to rush this story to Canada; I had it written in my mind, sequence after sequence.

Donato came to me: "I know what you're thinking, *amigo*. But what's the use, eh?" His tone was different, concerned. "Don't you understand what's taking place in Latin America? You must be on our side. It's why you came here to meet me. That's why I came here too in the first place." He looked pained; but it also seemed that there was the question of the myth associated with him: as he if he didn't want to go on.

Maybe he wasn't comfortable in this role.

He limped closer to me.

And at the end of that day Donato appeared weary, exhausted.

I decided to stay on, and he didn't mind. Sadie was also pleased. The night air was cool, refreshing, despite a faint scent of cow's urine.

A guitar played almost funereally, the whine of peasant songs. I looked out of my window...at the solitary moon, like the bloodshot eyes of a drunkard. Large, luminous: then opaquely drawn. Donato himself, I saw, outside–with the peasants.

I looked closer from my window. Donato himself started playing, the peasants around him, happy, singing along from time to time, and then their rhapsodic chants. Donato simply sang louder, more rhapsodic.

But I was getting tired, though I wanted to observe more closely what was going on. I also sensed Donato looking up at me once or twice; then, he seemed oblivious of me–though he waved, and it wasn't my imagination. And his loud laughter punctuated the long, empty night. A burro suddenly braying, far, distant; a horse also neighing as if in concatenation. Maybe I had fallen asleep and was dreaming. Montreal and Manazama were now one in an odd phantasmogoria; shapes and shadows, accusing, laughing; gleeful expressions. I started saying, "No, no," and got up, perspiring; now listening to the sounds of the men outside, Donato's drone. A guitar's further melancholy strains. Then–a vast emptiness, the Manazama night overwhelming all else.

The next morning Donato looked fresh as ever (though I was weary, a little exhausted). "It was wonderful last night," I attempted over breakfast.

He didn't reply.

"D'you often do that?"

"It was a victory."

"Victory?" I stopped eating.

"Yes, for the peasants I mean. High up in the mountains."

"You mean there was actually a battle?"

Sadie looked at me from beneath her long eyelashes.

"That's a story you will write about," he said next, looking at me. The gleam flashed again in his eyes. I became alert. "Maybe you will repay me with some discretion, Richard."

I assured him I would.

"When are you going back to Canada?" he asked, pointedly.

"I'm not sure...I have a few things to check out first."

He kept looking at me.

"The you will be returning to Montreal, won't you?"

"Yes."

"I have forgotten what Montreal looks like, you know."

"You mean, you haven't been back...in...?"

"Twenty-five years."

For some strange reason he suddenly laughed, and I also laughed. And it was as if Montreal no longer existed in either of our minds. Sadie was the only one who didn't laugh: to her Montreal was palpably real. Did she ever visit there? Later I found out that she did, it was there she first met Donato. At that moment he and I were suddenly one, true Canadians at heart. And it seemed my presence now took him back there; took him out of something, which the peasants all along had control over.

He continued laughing.

And all that I'd heard about Donato: everything, now disappeared; he was just an ordinary man, pudgy, overweight, a Canadian who happened to have wandered far. A little flaky, perhaps; who, instead of moving further north, came south.

Donato continued laughing, as if to say that the joke was really on me, and didn't I know?

"I told you you were different," he said amidst laughter.

"So are you," I mumbled, smiling.

He ignored my allusion.

He laughed again, hollowly this time.

I got up, ready to leave.

Donato wanted to drive me himself to the town. I insisted that his chauffeur would do. We affectionately embraced. Sadie managed a smile, though she was a little haughty as before. And, maybe, she was indeed glad to see me go.

From his window he waved, as the car sped off.

I laughed to myself. I told the driver that I wanted to drive past the electric train, which would be in motion on Monday...two days away.

"It's forbidden, Señor," the driver replied.

"What's forbidden?"

"To drive past the train."

"It cannot be," I let out impatiently.

"*Iss* our superstition, Señor," he tried to explain. "The train must be hidden from sight–from a stranger's sight, before it actually goes into motion. After the ceremony, that *iss*..."

"But I am a Canadian," I let out. "That train, it's a gift from the people of Canada."

"Oh, no, Señor, *iss* a gift from Señor Donato, only. *Iss* his train,see."

"What d'you mean?"

I ordered him to stop the car, and to explain in detail what he meant. He seemed a little frightened. "I thought you knew. You are his *amigo*, no?"

"I am so," I said, thinking hard.

The driver looked more relaxed. Then slowly he began telling me: that it was Donato who'd really bought the train from the Canadian Government for the people of Manazama. It was he who had designed it as well, one suited to the region, which had been hinted to me by my contact in the Department of External Affairs. I also recalled that Donato had come to the region as an engineer about twenty-five years ago and had decided to stay on. He'd been working on this train all these years; and now his dream was fulfilled; oddly, he was the one who'd decided to pander to their superstition...to satisfy their deepest longings, such was his devotion to the people of Manazama.

But why didn't Donato tell me all these things? Unless...he wanted me to think that he was really a simple man, to the very end. The driver started the car once more.

"That Señor Donato, you see, *iss* not even Canadian," he muttered, driving fast.

"What?"

"Montreal, ah, but what *iss* Montreal, eh? Just a city, well, a place like Manazama. Señor Donato lives here, he *iss* one of us; he lives here longer than he lived in Montreal, maybe."

The puzzlement on my face seemed ridiculous to him, as he smiled. I looked around, at the region: and he was laughing hard, a little like Donato himself. And in him, I saw all that I'd seen in Donato, that which belied his simplicity: which I had allowed to slip out of my grasp when I was close to him, my conceiving him as someone of abject ordinariness.

I knew then I couldn't write about him; not anymore. He was, well, too elusive; I had to know him far better. Only in my imagination perhaps would I keep seeing him the way I wanted to; and only when he was solidly in my mind, firmly sculpted... Then, one day, I'd attempt to write his story. For now, I'd return to Montreal...because of the exhaustion of my too-much travelling, thinking about him....And maybe I'd start from his boyhood: which would be my real apprenticeship!

# THREE

# AIN'T GOT NO CASH

There was something odd about Mamie the moment I set eyes on her. I was new to the Bronx, I told her so. Mamie looked curiously at me, as the others milled around the bar, mostly Puerto Rican types, some black, some white. In the interchanging dark and light the music playing, the band warming up; one member of it distinctly long-haired, he with dark glasses on. And everyone else kept talking, muttering, then occasionally laughing loudly.

Someone suddenly started calling himself Bongo Santamaria, and further laughter rose, quick, spasmodic. And Mamie, close to the bar, said to me:

"Maybe you like it here. It's diff'rent from Canada, see. You must get a green card. It's easy."

The music started throbbing, and fellas began swaying their hips, the night's pulsation, their own faces' heavy expression; sounds clapping against my ears.

But Mamie seemed all, her voice in me, the green card, something. "Yeah, I guess so," I replied in an offbeat way.

I was staying with a friend, Miro, maybe for a week. He was, well, always himself, laughing; same as when we were back home in Guyana. Miro, now in the swirling light, as Mamie concentrated, watching him out of the corner of her eyes, it wasn't hard to tell.

More sounds. Someone else entering, and calling out, "Hey, Miro, what's up, man?" In a way it was as if many voices were calling out at once; more of New York City, this hot August; frenzy all around.

And Miro was now talking in a back-slapping way to the one calling himself Bongo; all the while Mamie kept watching him, in this heart of the Burnside District, South Bronx. Now it seemed everyone was acting in a peculiar way. Mamie drew closer to me, sidling up almost; much closer. Heavy set, she was: extending from her stool to mine at the bar.

The barman smiled, talking to himself in strange tones. And Mamie's eyes seemed larger, as she looked from him to me (into me sort of). Ah, this Mamie, would I agree to her teaching me to dance Latin? Would I? I didn't reply, and she rattled on, "Maybe you can get a green card. You stay in America for good. You can work here for a while." Then she looked ruefully at me.

But she once more quickly turned to Miro: as if watching me through him; he—also watching me, then turning away, but quickly staring again, making an odd face, a sort of grotesquerie or parody, muscles bulging at his shirt sleeves. *Christ, Miro, what's up, man?* Miro was talking to the fellow in dark glasses; and in a way, he was pretending. I figured right then he could become an actor if he wanted. His mouth twitching, pretending to be angry, then happy as he playfully slapped the dark-glassed one, Bongo. And the band throbbed. Tenderness to livid rage in Miro's eyes, this most extraordinary thing happening; still the actor he was.

Mamie fidgeted.

And I kept thinking about Miro: as if Mamie was forcing me to do this, by the way she kept on fidgeting, muttering to herself. She glanced at Miro again. Ah, yes, Miro had been living in the Bronx for the last five years, and why didn't I visit him before I didn't know. He'd yelled at me over the phone for wanting to live in Canada, as if I had much choice in the matter. "Man, that place is cold!" It sounded frightening, the way he kept repeating this, the phone's static, protest: as I recalled the reason why we'd left Guyana. Voices in my head; Miro still berating me about Canada. And one thing was sure: we'd felt driven. As teenagers, Miro and I often watched re-runs of old American movies, lots of Bogart stuff: Miro, then, skinny as an eel, would shout loudly as if he'd suddenly gone mad: "Yeah, I'd like to go to America one day, man. Shit, I'd like to have all those nice-lookin' broads for my self!"

He was still with this Bongo fellow who was now slumped in a corner looking like a zombie. And over the years, I kept thinking, Miro was transformed, grown fat because of the booze and all the American junk food he ate. He'd lost most of the hair on his head too; which sometimes made him look, well, fierce when he scowled. And wily too he was from time to time, rolling up his sleeves, and laughing again, bellowing. As if he was still talking to me on the phone: that last time, all his boast about the Manhattan Psychiatric State Hospital, and his trying to organize the part-time workers into a trade union. "I could raise hell, man. Yes, they're mostly Blacks an' Latinos, see. They need organizing. Shit, with a union I could bust management ass. Even Governor Mario Cuomo would take notice of me then!"

But with Miro, nothing ever got off the ground, because ideas flitted in and out of mind just like that; and now, no doubt he was telling the fellow in dark glasses about his new scheme, some new idea: which, later, he'd tell me about also.

"He, your friend?" Mamie asked, sensing where my attention was.

"Who?" as if I didn't know.

"That one." Her voice, hard.

"Yes." I smiled.

"I've seen him around."

"Oh?"

"Yes, lotsa time." Mamie was looking straight at him, boring holes into him.

"You could be mistaken."

She kept looking at him.

"He doesn't come here often," I offered. "It's his first time." That was what Miro had said to me.

Mamie shrunk away from me: she with a thick crop of kinky hair; her thick glasses added to the penetrating quality of her eyes holding me like clamps.

Casually sort of, I started telling her of an experience I had earlier that day as I tried using the pubic telephone. It was about this dude, mean-looking as hell, who kept hugging the phone to himself for more than an hour; whispering into it, talking to himself, only. Mamie, her clamps still on me. Yes, I'd been lost coming back from Manhattan on the A train, and I wanted to call Miro to tell him about my whereabouts; I needed help.

Mamie said New York has a way of doing things like that to people; to strangers; that was why I needed to get a green card. Cheeks flushed, as she added:

"I don't like him."

"The dude?"

"No, him–that one, your friend." She pointed, with her eyes.

"Oh?" I was disappointed.

"You shouldn't be staying with him." She almost winced.

"But I've known him for years. We grew up together, Miro an' me. We're like brothers." I didn't like the way Mamie was trying to drive a wedge between us. But it was her way, her eyes, getting under my skin. But she was still close to me, large-bosomed as she was. Then, something soft about her, reaching out to me. She asked me my name, because I hadn't told her before we met at the bar, unpredictably. Everyone called me Sylvio, I said.

"Okay, Sylvio," she replied, "you like women?"

"What?"

Music—the drums' heavy beat-throbbing. Outside, the pallid air, whirling. Torrents of feelings. Miro still with Bongo, but looking at us, his own eyes' hardness.

"Women—you like them?"

Here in the heart of the South Bronx, the buildings seeming at an angle, highrises, all roach-infested. So I heard; so Miro had said earlier that day; and would Mamie confirm this now? My thinking of Canada, snow and ice most of the year round: in the Eskimo-wilderness of space; my own limitless boundaries, defining my immigrant self in eelgrass, wide lakes and rivers. This Turtle Island, a Mohawk's or Ojibwa's.

I shrugged. Maybe I like women.

"Let's dance," she mutttered. "I will teach you Hispanic moves. You're not Hispanic, you know. You don't look Hispanic to me."

I played along, and we stepped into the middle where everyone else had started dancing, the air metallic with the drums' frenzy. After a while, we seemed alone in the torrid air; everyone else watching. We were only a few feet away from Miro. Mamie said she really wanted to have a good look at him.

Miro also watching Mamie, wasn't he? Amidst the interchanging dark and light, like chiaroscuro, the air's folly. Mamie held me closely; as if I actually belonged to her. In her ears' whir: and she said next that I should move my legs between hers, slowly: it was the way to do it, to dance, the slow beat; yes, feel the rhythm: Canada was miles away, like another planet. Ah, I was still an alien. Her breath hot; she was still chiding.

"Just listen to the music, an' move your legs, slowly. Yeah, like that. No. Come on—you can do it." Slowly: something between a man and a woman only, she said. Mamie seemed as if she was controlling the musicians, the Latin band playing, all their faces before me. Miro's too, everywhere; he, talking to the drummer, then to Bongo once more, who laughed giddily.

Mamie added, "You're doing well, Sylvio. Maybe you'll stay in the Bronx. Yeah, you will stay with me; with big Mamie, no?" Her tongue darted out, wetting my left ear.

Laughter. Miro's?

I held Mamie closely, and concentrated on the music; my legs between hers, the sensations creeping up in me; as Mamie added:

"The blacks own this part of town. It's the way it should be. See, I am black also: I don't have to tell you that." The light suddenly shining, dispensing with the dark. "Yeah, it don't matter though, black or not."

Her hot breath still against my ears as we danced. Next she laughed, but once more she looked at Miro, looking through my neck, boring holes into my skin.

"Say, can you love a woman?" I heard, in a fashion, her knees fastened between my legs. When the music stopped, it was as if she willed it. "Take me home with you, Sylvio," she added; the light in the bar dimmed considerably. We seemed to have been dancing for an hour. Smoke swirling; while I kept thinking about Mamie, the way she was easily attaching herself–to a guy–to me. When she smiled, her teeth whitely shone.

"Ah, I was just trying you out," she said, almost with guile, grinning.

She gulped her drink once more by the bar.

I quickly ordered another, and kept looking at her.

"Don't get me wrong," she added. "I know lotsa guys; all of them come here too. That Bongo, you see he's watching me. Yeah, he'll soon leave, but he's also pretending: they're all pretending. That's how it is in this part of town." She was looking at Miro again, as if she didn't know what else to say or do. Then strangely hesitant she grew. As Bongo started walking out–just as Mamie said he would. She really intrigued me now.

She continued, with a distinct drawl: "Yeah, we have a good time in this neighborhood–the Blacks an' the Hispanics. We're really one people. But we don't always act like it. Yeah, same roots in slavery; but we don't act like it." She half-scowled, continuing: "It's the pretending that gets to me. Don't get me wrong, I like whites too. My husband, you see, he was a honkie; but we couldn't make it together after a while; we were poles apart."

She laughed lightly, as if embarrassed to say this, the smoke filling the room. "It took me three long years to realize that; and all the time, you know, he kept insisting he was Hispanic," she added.

Then, Miro coming forward; maybe he wanted to warn me about something. It was now one o' clock; maybe he was eager to leave, it being so late: the same Miro who was known to stay out all night.

Mamie swallowed smoke-filled air, and was about to start coughing.

"Say, aren't you gonna take me home?" she asked.

"Take you home?"

"Yeah." She yawned, a little voluminously; and maybe she was pretending herself, eyes softening now when she smiled.

Then I knew–Miro wanted me to split with Mamie. But I reflected on our dance a few moments ago, the way her legs touched mine, sensations in my body, tremors (in a way). And Mamie's wonderful fragrance, I was still breathing her. My looking at her, taking her hand, close to the counter, squeezing–almost squeezing her mass of flesh. Hot flesh. Warmth of her mouth–the roundness, abundance of her face, cheeks, ear lobes. Yes–you–Mamie, all there was about you, in the waning light. Ah Miro, what are you thinking?

I said to her that I didn't mind taking her home.

She smiled: tremor of lips. Then, she muttered: "This is a rough neighborhood, Sylvio. You be careful." Looking at me: "Yeah, I like it here though." She continued squeezing my hand, adding:

"I teach sometimes, see; I thought of teaching regularly, but I never really got around to it. Lots of other things I need doing around here, in this neighborhood."

Suddenly she looked across at Miro. "Him," she growled–"I don't like."

Miro was now telling me–urgently–it was time to go.

Mamie quietly linked her arm into mine. "I can't stay here much longer. Come on, let's go."

"Where...are we going?"

"To your place," she almost snapped.

"Mine?"

"Yeah."

I looked at her with slight awe, Mamie–commanding now - having her way. I felt I was about to be swallowed up by her, once more. But, again, she was talking about the neighbourhood, the music starting once more. Others getting up to dance. Sway and whirl. Voices in my head. Fragrances. And faroff places, the tropics' own; contrasting with Canada's snowy whiteness. Miro was now dancing, this time with an attractive darkhaired woman with huge, sad-looking Hispanic eyes, their movements becoming swift, jerky, yet grand as she followed him around the floor, whirling even more. And all the while Mamie's eyes were on him. The dancers' panting, then laughing, wide-mouthed: Miro grinning from ear to ear; his muscles rippling, perspiring; he seemed to extend from wall to wall, reaching out to us, me–still a warning? And the darkhaired Hispanic woman's further leap and stride, flaming red, so slim-waisted!

Then Miro seemed to forget all about me as he leant closer to her, focusing on her sad face, sombre yet large, luminous eyes. She was engrossed in him also; and I figured a woman often excited him that way: he who'd accused me of living a sheltered life in Canada. Come over to America, man, he'd urged: the phone dangling in my hand. He'd been divorced a couple of times already. Arms and legs extending, more and more. And Mamie, oddly, kept being glued to him, despite all the while still muttering about the neighborhood, like leitmotif. And was she, this Hispanic one, from this district also?

"Sure," said Mamie, "Blacks have got to learn to respect themselves, each other. I'm all for them taking positive action to better themselves. But it must start with self-awareness. Without it, there's no hope; no hope for the community."

She swallowed hard, still glued to Miro; then, "Nothing else seems to change people here, you understand."

"Are we leaving?" I asked. I was starting to get bored in a way; though my thoughts were still on Miro, our going to his place. Oddly, it was as if I now wanted to get away from Miro; and from this neighborhood, maybe, rough as it was. Christ, Mamie, do you have to tell me all this now?

"There's no time to waste," she murmured, the light almost bristling; the dancers' rhythmic moves, again and again; like our own thoughts, the band's own somersault. Miro's eyes, his arms extending to her bare back–firmly placed there.

The Bronx night greeted us with drug-pushers, pimps; drunks lingering, leaning against doorposts and pissing, jet-streamed; the ramshackle air and pulse in our tottering walk. But when Mamie took my arm, all seemed stable: the night itself belonged to her.

She began talking of a conference she'd organized for unwed mothers. There were too many kids around without fathers, who'd soon grow up to be adults yearning for the torrid night life (same as ourselves); other cravings. Crack and coke. Yes, it was a kind of revenge, or the energy of assault. A surreal neighborhood. And Mamie wanted to do something about it. Our walking slowly, in the fetid night air, urine-scented, like miasma of a sort. A chain rattling somewhere, one leg dragged along. Who was it? Christ, who really cared? Miro?

Next Mamie said she didn't believe in rage. "I don't want to sound like a social worker, or be cynical, you see," she added. "I much prefer people evolving in their own own space, no matter how slow it is. It's how it ought to be with black people, you understand."

Mamie continued on, sometimes in a kind of mystical manner, unclear; yet very determined. A Pinto screeched noisily not far from where a drunk staggered and swore in response; like rapid gunfire. Sounds bringing me back to the present, to Mamie's words, my own palpable fear.

"Yeah," she added, my arm in hers, "it'd be easier if the children weren't born bastards."

I looked at her.

She whirled forward, as if jolted by a surprising thought: all her own; and maybe she'd drunken too much. And the ones lurking, looking at us, the chain dragging along, the street's own silent evocation. When another car screeched, I seemed to expect it and instinctively put my hands to my ears. Someone let out an explosive laugh, like more gunfire.

But Mamie laughed, her tongue stretching out as if oddly fanning the air. She added:

"You could stay here, forever–if you want. Yeah, I have a child, and I want my child to grow up in this neighborhood, decent, see."

She rambled on, in a fashion: "You understand, Sylvio: it's a good place here; you'd like it before long. Ignore the guys, the ones you see in the dark, there–look at them. Maybe you can't see them the way I do. It's nothing else for them to do. One maybe, a special one, he's watching you; watching us all. Maybe it has something to do with our heritage." She breathed in heavily before adding: "You see, it's important to keep loving them."

Mamie sounded unlike herself, her mind's own incessant hum the more she talked. I figured she was now on some kind of a crusade, and I was her wiling-unwilling convert.

She took my arm closer to her as we kept up the pace; all the while still telling me about the Bronx, this Burnside district, the cockroachy, spindly-legged life of small apartments oozing a silent invisible blood. The dark's shutters. Then her smile, like further light; a moment's embrace.

The key was on the ledge where Miro had left it (for me– he'd said). The rickety stairs, six storeys high. And Mamie didn't say much now. She only watched me, aware of my movements. Silent, apprehensive, we both were. A large bottle of cheap Italian wine and Scotch reached out to us from the living room table. Mamie at once poured herself a drink, as if it was the most natural thing in the world for her to do. And when we kissed, her perfume, amidst the odour of Scotch and wine, seemed all; the moments' meeting, with lips and hands, fumbling.

She chortled, then impulsively pulled back. But she was speaking again: she said it was good–really good–that I came to New York. And one day, maybe, she'd come to Toronto; she'd thought about it many times; but Canada was really honkie country, wasn't it? The Bronx was her world, her neighborhood; lurking fears and all. "It's part me, you understand," she added, her lips wet and glistening. My face now buried in her neck, and she caressed my head, and kept on talking: "You don't have to leave New York, you see." I fumbled with her clothes.

"It's something between a man and a woman maybe," she added.

Then suddenly she became tense. She held my right hand, the arrested air.

"What's the matter?"

"It's him..."

"Who?"

"Your friend–"

"Miro?"

"Yeah."

"What about him?"

"I can hear him."

"Really?"

She nodded.

"You're imagining, Mamie," I said, my face again on her neck.

"He's close by. Just listen."

"I am listening."

"You're not. It's important to listen. Listening's all."

I listened. Really.

"He's close by, I tell you."

No, Mamie. But I listened, or pretended to for a while. And the heaviness of the Bronx night came to me more fully, the dim stars, also; and maybe now, the morning was slowly starting out. And sun and clouds; or faraway tropical sunshine, the place where Miro and I had grown up; palpable as jewelry, in a sense.

"Let's get on with it," I urged, my impatience growing; and–oddly–tiredness.

But Mamie would have none if it; she expected Miro to burst in on us at any moment: the same Miro who an hour or so ago was dancing, as if a strange madness had overtaken him. He still with his Hispanic woman. Where had he met her? She seemed to symbolize all of the Big Apple, yet didn't. Only Mamie was; and she kept looking at the door, anxious.

Yes, it was Miro alright; Mamie became tense.

He entered, and said not a word. Only his silence, gloomy, the night air with him, reeking. He walked past us. Mamie remained deathly quiet.

Miro heaved, hard.

Mamie, I figured, felt like a trapped animal. And suddenly I was beginning to feel the same way. The entire apartment, with Miro a part of it, was keeping us contained.

Suddenly I wished Miro hadn't come home. I wished too Mamie wasn't acting like this, a bunched knot or spring ready to uncoil, unleash.

She whispered, "It's getting late. I...should never have come."

"It's still early," I said.

From his room, the only one in the apartment, Miro made a heavy, distinct sound; he was letting us know he was still present. His unmistakeable way undoubtedly: his rage, and distance.

Mamie's eyes widened, and she became even more uneasy, buttoning her blouse. "I must go," she repeated. "Don't keep me here any longer."

She kept saying this with every act, every expression. "Take me home–you must," she urged, in a further whisper. The Bronx night, like a bigger spring now; and those ones in the neighborhood, lurking, a plethora of chains dragging along, each with clamps, hooks. And what did Mamie say? Yes, learn to love them.

I became restless; Miro so close by: yet, not from this neighborhood. He was at the same time not from the tropics. We never were, in a sense, I figured.

Mamie's eyes suddenly blazed. "You must take me home. You brought me here." And the entirety of the Bronx was expressing itself in her.

But Mamie, I was silently saying, I don't dare walk back with you; not out there alone! Night's anxieties in me now more than ever, a complete stranger as I was–feeling stranger by the minute.

"You're in my neighborhood," she said, firmly. And she looked incredulously at me. She hissed next, "You must take me home!"

"It's very late, Mamie. Why not...stay the night?" I offered, my further invitation, welcoming.

Mamie cast a glance in the direction of Miro's room. And her round face turned angular; as if at that moment Miro appeared before us, looming. And he threatened her as no man ever did. And it was as if Miro, suddenly, was a part of me, the place we'd grown up in, the same village, country, all of it flooding into me. And only Mamie was the stranger.

"Please, you must understand," I muttered when I caught myself. "You can stay the night."

"I don't trust him," she hissed again. "It's a thing I have, understanding men. The way I do, maybe..."

I took her hand, caressing her.

But Mamie was now doing a disappearing act on me; she wasn't with me at all. She was almost stiff, suddenly a ball of wax.

"I will not stay; it's your fault I am here. Take me home," she pressed.

We argued; then finally, unable to cope with me any longer–I'd worn her patience, all her love–she said:

"Okay, give me the money, I will take a taxi."

I hesitated. And maybe it was Miro in me–talking to me from the other room.

Mamie got up.

I figured right then she didn't want to go any longer. Her eyes ablaze; and she was looking directly at Miro's room; and maybe she felt--as much as I–that he would indeed burst out upon her, us–at any moment.

She looked at me again, this time muttering something about her child being without a father. Softly repeating this; this neighbourhood still being all. "This friend o' yours," she added, in a hush, "he's not one of us. I know how it feels to come from here." She swallowed hard, as if it pained her to say this.

"But you are." I was? "You will return here. Maybe you don't belong to Canada either."

She looked sadly at me; and I figured this was what she wanted to say all along.

I mulled over her words amidst the taxi's hum and whir; the long, winding night, the streets' circuitous welcoming of her. She indeed had to go, dialling at the phone; the door bell soon after buzzing. Mamie looking back at me. Maybe I really didn't belong to Canada.

And how I longed to be some place with Mamie: she still with me, going along the circuitous route, like a maze. Then getting out of the taxi, and walking up the stairs to her apartment. Eyes watching her from crevices, jalousies. A baby screaming.

I kept feeling a wave of regret.

"You liked her, didn't you?" asked Miro, taking me by surprise at the door. "The way you danced with her, so close." He convulsed with a quick laugh.

"Yeah," I said.

"That woman, she's strange."

"Not stranger than you, Miro," I said, with some heat, also convulsing.

"There's many like her."

I grimaced.

"Take my word for it."

I turned, looking at him.

"Ah," he said, straightening up in dignified control, despite alcohol reeking from his breath; and it was Miro's new side, intriguing me no end.

I muttered, "She knew you, she said. She'd seen you many times before."

He shrugged, and growled, savouring the right time to reply to me. Typical Miro, I thought; the door still ajar, loud banging from somewhere, in other parts of the building. Doors closing, reopening, night's or morning's welcoming rite.

"She's concerned about this neighborhood," I added. "She knows it intimately."

He scoffed. "You're infatuated with her."

I denied this, though my thoughts were still with the way we'd danced, the softer music, night's rhythms.

Miro sat down on the beige couch in the growing light of the morning streaming in through the main window.

"So you're leaving today–to go back to Canada?" he asked.

I'd almost forgot about it, I was still thinking about Mamie. Next I was thinking about her in a Toronto street: it wasn't New York anymore.

Miro eyed me, in an angle of sharper light.

"Maybe," I muttered, not looking at him. In a way, I was hoping--suddenly–that I wasn't leaving.

"You can stay longer," he offered; then, like an afterthought: "The Bronx's a strange place; it can grow on you."

He yawned.

"I don't know why I settled here." He looked at me, as if I would provide the answer. He yawned again. "Why we both had to leave there, eh?"

He went on like this, nostalgia in him, his feelings–the way he talked.

I figured he wanted to go back to his room, but out of some strange duty he had to keep talking to me.

He yawned again...

While I recalled our past, why we'd really left. Why Guyana drove us away. Indeed why too North America pulled us to it, like a magnet. My thoughts also traveled back to Mamie: she still in the taxi and driving round and round the neighbourhood...and the ones watching her all the time. Who were they really?

Miro now started talking about his scheme that had to do with the Manhattan Psychiatric State Hospital. And it was then he said where he'd first seen Mamie.

He grinned, and yawned again almost simultaneously.

No, he wasn't making this up. It was Mamie alright, and she'd recognized him.

"There's a kind of madness living here, New York City–you see. Being away from where we came from, maybe. It is," he affirmed.

He was being sentimental now, and yawned again.

All the while I kept thinking about Mamie. "Why didn't you warn me?" I asked.

"Warn you?" He seemed surprised.

"Yes."

"With Mamie, it's difficult," he said. "You know, she's changed a lot over the years." His thoughts wandered. "Lots of guys around here have changed too." He looked at me, as if in doubt. "They all know her; they know about her. Maybe she's told you things she's done, the community work."

"She said to love...them."

Miro smiled."Ah yes, that too."

His expression was forlorn, one I hadn't seen in him in a long time.

And he yawned again.

"Maybe she doesn't trust me."

"Maybe." I looked him fully in the eyes.

He turned away.

He added, "That Mamie, maybe she trusts no man. It's her way, maybe."

He seemed really tired now, though his eyes were wide open.

"It's always been like that with her. But she'll change. They do--they all do...these patients. There's no place for them there anymore; they have to come home."

He paused, then slowly added, "No doubt she can explain it better."

"She really thinks you don't belong to the Bronx" I said in defence.

"I do." He looked away from me. I figured he'd once more start talking about his special scheme.

Just then I thought I saw the two of them together; their meeting again at the Manhattan Psychiatric State Hospital and planning a strategy to organise a union against all odds. And it wasn't the Hispanic woman dancing with him at the bar--but Mamie, beautiful, voluptuous; she, whirling with him, yet keeping her distance. And their coming to grips with each other, a reconciliation--and only I was the real outsider.

Or wasn't I?

Maybe, too, with them it was something between a man and a woman. And I recalled Mamie's words to me; each phrase: I was listening carefully to her now.

My eyes closed.

"She's no doubt at home now," Miro said quietly, breaking my thoughts. "Maybe fast asleep. We shouldn't be up at this time. You'll be traveling this afternoon, no?"

But it was he who I was worried about, though I didn't say this. Just then, I figured we were two entirely different beings who'd never grown up together. And now we weren't even apart.

Again Miro yawned. "Maybe I shouldn't be here at all, Sylvio. Not in the Bronx I mean."

He closed his eyes on the couch, as if he'd fallen asleep.

When I thought he actually did, he opened his eyes again. "That Mamie," he muttered, "all the others–they learn to take care of themselves. It's the only way; wherever you are." He closed his eyes sombrely. "Maybe you will want to come here again." He grinned.

I continued thinking about Mamie, even when Miro returned to his room. Mamie's special feeling between a man and a woman; something of an unexpressed embrace; her presence still lingering. And I knew that back in Canada, I'd be thinking about her. And when Miro phoned again, I would hear in him the voice of the tropics no longer. And Mamie, yes–wherever she'd be, she'd continue to bring us–Miro and me–together, oddly enough. My thinking about this; and Mamie cuddling her child and muttering: "You've got to love them."

Maybe she meant me as well.

# A PLAN IS A PLAN

Is a funny thing with certain fellas when they see a black man walking down the street with a white chick. Immediately they'd start eyeballing him. Well, I guess that ain't too surprising 'cause most of the time these fellas only grown up seeing black people being by themselves on the islands, with white people as tourists or managers on the sugar-estates, or simply being big executives driving around in fancy cars or motor cycles - all of which they might have read about or seen on TV. So they're marvellin' now when they see a poor arse black man having a white thing leaning on his shoulder. Another thing, too: many of these same black fellas spending all their time at a disco, trying to pick up a white thing, as if that's all that matters in life as soon as they come to Canada.

I guess it's the same with my friend Roland, who used to be one of the shyest fellas around, spending all his time behind books; then once he started going to the discos...bam! He change! Now he's no longer spending day and night dreaming of becoming a doctor as he uses to do on the island before coming to Canada. Roland's a different cat now: he's spending all the money he has on fancy clothes, looking really well-dressed like the smartest cat around. Sometimes I'd wonder where Roland got all the money from. You see, Roland's full of guile, too. For instance, upon seeing me, he smiles widely as if he was born with that smile on his face; as if, too, to say that money is as easy to come by, as if it comes into a man's pocket like manna from heaven... once a man arrives in Canada! I guess also it's because this time he has his blonde chick leaning on his shoulder while he's looking up at the sky like master an' king all in one!

I figure that Roland's really workin' hard, or how else could he be wearing the fancy three-piece suit he has on now, gallivantin' around with his chick for other fellas to gawk an' stare at and muttering that he, Roland, is one helluva lucky fella; that God really blesses some folks, black as they are!

Roland, seeing me, waves - just a little wave mind you, his head held high up, reserved sort of, like he's one special dude. An' it's all on account o'this chick. I sayin' to myself, Roland, you'll suffer because of her. Wait an' see! But I dare not tell him this to his face 'cause Roland, suave as he looks now, could become really ignorant all of a sudden when island-madness takes over, which is a strange thing, too. I imagine Roland swearing at me--a thing he never uses to do, 'cause he used to be a God-fearing, non-swearing Christian boy back home, thanks to his serious-minded holier-than-thou mother.

But I'm still saying to myself that Roland's in for a hard time all on account o' this chick.

Other fellas looking at Roland and thinking the same thing. I notice a couple of white cats along the street eyeing him now. I guess they're saying that a black fella has no right going out with a white chick - especially one as blonde as she--because the races were never meant to mix - as if that's written in holy ink itself. I guess, too, some fellas think they're still in places in the far south of the US of A where they have folks running around with white sheets over their heads and joining up with neo-Nazis an' such like who are interested in the purity of the human race. Which race it is, is a different matter, I say!

I also say some fellas don't understand that opposites tend to attract each other. I mean, a really black dude could be stronger attraction for a blonde-white thing 'cause that's how nature works sometimes, if you understand what I'm getting at. Besides, there's something really colourful about it, too (pardon me!). Don't get me wrong: it's Roland I'm really concerned about; after all a friend's a friend --way he holds on to the chick and waves.

So, I'm telling myself that Roland must be some sort of a stubborn mule. But what if the fella's really in love? Yeah, I guess it's no sweet island-thing for him now as he uses to say, talking all the time about only going out with women who have the sun deep in their skin and laughter in their bones which maketh the earth to blush. No siree! My boy Roland now prefers a woman white like chalk, whose blood is pure ice by the looks of it, who could lift her head high up in the air, hardly looking down or around--but looking only uppish! What surprises me, too, is how such a classy woman could fall for a fella like Roland. Don't get me wrong - Roland's not an ugly cat (definitely not one o' them *orangutans* I see idling around sometimes at Selwynn's Bar). He's a handsome dude, especially now in his fancy suit. But Christ, something else about that blonde makes her different, that puts her in a class all her own.

I guess Roland doesn't realize this yet as he holds on to her, putting his arm about her waist and pulling her tightly to himself while looking all moony-eyed and love-lorn.

Other fellas still looking and talking.

"He sure is the luckiest guy around," I hear one say.

"I wish I was as lucky as he," declares another. "I mean, to have a thing like that leaning on my arm. Imagine him on top of her. It's bound to be like sweet heaven!"

The others laugh.

"Is a black ram tupping a white ewe!" another burst out. I thought then that this fella has a classical frame of mind, quoting Shakespeare like this as if he's familiar with great learning, even though I know for sure he hasn't been further than Grade Nine. But we's fellas is like that sometimes - full of surprises, if you know what I mean, 'cause I hearin' these same fellas quoting the Bible and the classics all in the same breath, which men with a string of degrees behind their names can't do.

I keep thinking about this as I'm heading for home. I'm thinking, too, that I'd be seeing Roland the next day, and he'd be telling me everything about this chick. Maybe he'd even boast a little. What gall and guile that man now possesseth!

I saying to Roland, "You better be careful, brother."

Roland eyes me sort of, then smiles; I guess he knows what I'm thinking. He says, "Don't worry, man, Suzan's just a piece o' tail." Well, to tell you the truth, I was surprised to hear talk like this cause I done believe that he's madly in love; but now it's as if this chick is nothing better than a hooker or some such.

"It's the truth, man," Roland grins.

"But Roland!"

"Don't worry, man. Suzan is fun, too. I mean, I could do anything I want with her." Roland laughs now, crazy sort of, as if he's in some kind of a fit - you know how some people can laugh so much they can't stop; some even dying like this. Well, Roland is in one of these fits right now. Suddenly I'm afraid for him, cause I'm wondering what a silly way it would be for a man to die, especially a fella like Roland. Just imagine the word getting back to the island: and people wondering how such a healthy fella like Roland passing away on account of laughter and wondering what a strange place this Canada must be.

"You sure, Roland?" I press, serious.

"Yeah, man. Suzan don't mind at all. I mean, she's in for all the fun I could give her."

"But...I mean, Roland...she's different!" I reply, cause right then I'm thinking what a really beautiful woman she is. "She's someone you could fall in love with" - I guess I wasn't sure what I was really saying.

Roland claps me on the shoulder, as if I was the strange one now, saying that I don't seem to know much about women, even though I'm a few years older than he - and better educated too! I mean, I've been attending evening classes right here; it's not like a man being born in Barbados and not being rich enough to afford going to a proper school.

"No, man, I'm not in love with Suzan."

"What about marriage?" I press quietly.

Roland is about to kill himself with laugh. "She isn't the marrying sort. Yeah, neither of us is the marrying kind," Roland saying, his mouth opening and closing like clothes flapping on the line.

"Really?" I ask, astonished sort of, and looking at Roland as if I'm seeing an entirely different fella. It's incredible how all this is happenin', all this being the result of his meeting this blonde. Christ! I'm having a helluva hard time figuring out Roland now. Just then he says he has to go 'cause he's meeting Suzan for lunch and he doesn't want to be late! In vain I mutter, "What's the matter, Roland? I mean, you don't have time for me anymore! Remember how we used to play dominoes every afternoon!"

Roland walks off, waving to me now as if I am miles away, saying he'll give me a ring, when I done know that I am the one who will have to do that; to hear him tell me, "Hold on a minute, man. Suzan's here. I guess I'm busy right now. Could you call another time..!"

I watch him running off, looking really happy too.

Right then I suspect that Roland's madly in love; but that he's really trying to put me off the trail. It's gotta be! How else could he be acting like this. No siree, I could see through Roland's guile. And at the same time I'm thinking of Brother Selwynn, wondering how he feels about all this, cause he too has Roland's interest at heart; at least that's what he says.

But as I keep thinking about this, I am suddenly more suspicious than ever.

So I find m'self heading for Selwynn's Bar on Spadina cause that's where a lot of cats hang out. Selwynn, a big, bearded Jamaican dude, is trying to prove to everyone that black people too could collect money from across the counter.

I see a bunch of other fellas there playing dominoes. Sometimes that's all they're doing: playing and talking politics at the same time, especially since the police in Toronto are now killing black people at the wink of an eye while City Hall's suggesting all kinds of solutions to the racial problem. I remember Selwynn once saying that it was all our fault, that the police are merely trying to keep law and order (it was then that Selwynn revealed that he was once a policeman in Kingston, Jamaica before coming to Canada). Maybe Selwynn's right, I keep thinking; our people should change their behaviour; black people shouldn't be playing loud music and laughing loudly without regard for others, as if they're back in the islands where they could do as they like; after all Canadian people are different, more reserved sort of. I am just in time to hear Selwynn making another suggestion to heal the 'racial wounds' as he calls it, telling the other dudes that intermarriage is the best sort of thing, cause before long there'd be so many chocolaty children running around the streets no one would be able to separate one race from another; yeah, it won't be as easy a matter as separatin' sheep from goats!

Immediately I'm thinking of Roland. Maybe he's one step ahead of the rest of us. Maybe he's really working for better racial harmony, socializin' in the best possible manner, and in a real classy way, too. I feel like telling the cats about Roland now.

But Selwynn greets me. "Man, I'm glad to see you," he says, laughing in his usual Selwynn-manner and talking even more loudly about his "plan"; right then I want to tell him that Roland, my buddy, is far ahead in this plan of action, despite my doubt cause once more I'm thinking of Roland getting into some sort of trouble: I mean, it's still hard to believe that a fella like Roland would want to spend all his hard-earned cash buying fancy suits and ignoring his studies. I mean, too, it won't get our people anywhere; that's what Selwynn oughta be talking about now, not intermarriage!

I decided to tell Selwynn and the others this, that this plan wouldn't work at all; that racial mixing was never known to work. But bearded Selwynn is sounding like an intellectual now, cop an' all that he was, and telling the others it would!

"Yeah, look at Roland, man. How come he's doing it?" Selwynn challenges when he senses my doubt.

"Yeah, how come?" the others chime.

I notice a few Rasta fellas present this time, whom I'd never seen before. Their eyes too are gleaming, imbued as everyone else is with this idea.

But I continue to protest, cause I am convinced that the plan wouldn't work; that Roland is having problems. To my surprise, Roland walks in right then, his woman all dressed up in a sexy sort of way, her eyes mascaraed, and her lips red like flame-flower so that she's looking more colourful than one of them Guyana toucans.

Roland smiling, too, looking more handsome than ever. Is strange what love could do to a man, I'm thinking. I notice all the fellas looking closely at the chick, really envying Roland. I guess they're even more eager to discuss racial harmony now, especially when they see this blonde thing smiling as if she was born with a smile on her face, chewing gum and still smiling as if she's a sweet angel from heaven.

I begin to feel silly sort of, cause I am the only one disagreeing now. The chick too is looking at me and still smiling and chewing gum, occasionally blowing it at me, which causes the others to laugh. Roland laughs loudest too, cause he's proud as hell...what for? It's not too hard to tell.

"It's gonna work," says Selwynn, his eyes bright as neon. The others chorus approval. And while the chick is still chewing gum and looking around indifferently sort of, Selwynn starts echoing a long-forgotten Kitchener or Sparrow calypso as if now to impress everyone.

I look at the blonde smiling and then blowing out more gum as she turns to look at Selwynn, causing the other fellas to burst out laughing again. But Roland, being a smart fella - especially when it comes to women - leads his chick out by the arm, 'cause he done realizes that Selwynn's eyes are canting each time the chick wriggles her endowments - as if for his satisfaction only. I quickly say to m'self, she's bound to cause trouble. But Selwynn's tongue stretches out like a salivating dog as he still looks at her and attempts to blow gum himself. "Give poor Roland a chance, man," Selwynn says loudly, then not so loudly while the Rasta fellas laugh loudly again.

"But Roland shoulda be sticking to his books - not tryin' to be a playboy in Canada," I counter. "Foolin' around and showin' off like that, wasting his poor mother's hard-earned cash which she's been sending to him ever so often!" In a way I am incensed now.

I left Selwynn's place, 'cause I couldn't get this thing solved; maybe I'm thinking too much of Roland's welfare, I tell m'self. So I press on, deciding to mind m'own business.

For days after I still am thinking about Roland and his girlfriend; I've been thinking, too, of Selwynn's plans, which the more I think about the more I am now beginning to feel would work. Maybe Roland's well on his way to becoming one hell of a successful man. I wasn't sure why I felt this way; I guess I'm thinking positively as I'd heard Roland once say. With this realization I find myself going down Spadina to tell Selwynn that I've had a change of heart.

Upon hearing me, Selwynn smiles, tapping me on the shoulder. "I knew you'd think the way we do," he says. I guess I begin looking around for Roland just then; but there's no sign of him; maybe he's busy with his blonde. And I don't blame him! By the looks of it I can tell that other fellas are also anxious about Roland; maybe they simply want to watch Suzan blowing out more gum. Even Selwynn, who's the oldest of us, is feeling the same way - I can tell - as he scratches his beard.

A week later Roland surprises everyone by walking in alone.

"Where's Suzan, man?" three or four fellas ask at the same time.

Roland looks glum, shaking his head like a horse, and not answering.

Selwynn, now more concerned than ever before, quickly goes up to him. "Tell us, man!"

"We broke up," let out Roland, still glum.

"What for?" presses Selwynn.

It's my turn. "Why don't you tell us what happened?" I notice Roland looking really depressed in a way I've never seen before.

Roland still remains quiet.

I continue to press him - as all the others huddle around.

"Why, eh?" I ask.

Roland, still looking down, says reluctantly, "She's gone off with some rich dude driving a Corvette! I should've known all along" - he sounded bitter.

"Known what?"

"That I shouldnt' have taken her seriously!"

"But you didn't Roland!" I remind him.

Roland ignores me. "Man, that chick borrowed a hundred and fifty dollars from me - money I received from my aunt who sent it from Barbados! An' now she's gone with it all; I can't even pay the rent for this month! I guess," he was looking at Selwynn, then at me, "I'd have to borrow from one of you fellas - "

Selwynn turns away right then. Roland looks steadfastly at me; I could tell he's swearing under his breath. He no longer looks handsome now. Christ, a man can change so easily - just like that, all on account of a woman!

I turn to Selwynn who's pouring a draft of his own beer for himself, guzzling it down like a man in a hurry. Roland stretches out for a glass, but Selwynn ignores him.

"We've got to continue this harmony thing," said Selwynn, wiping his largish mouth and glaring at Roland, then looking at the Rasta cats with their dreadlocks an' all. "One bad apple doesn't spoil the entire barrel," he announces sort of. I feel like laughing then, but restrain myself.

Roland looks around foolishly. Suddenly he says, "Yeah, man, it's a personal thing! Suzan and I" - he doesn't say more; he's still bitter.

The others turn around and look at each other. Then at Selwynn, who still keeps insisting that racial mixing is very important. But Roland, as if to himself, adds, "I done say it's a personal thing. See what Suzan's done to me: you can't trust a woman! And there's plenty like her -that's what my aunt Edna would say if I were to tell her this...Yeah, she was right - never trust anyone these days! Not even your best friend." Roland is sounding very bitter now, and I begin to feel really sorry for him. His face is deeply drawn, and I figure maybe he was genuinely in love with her. How could he not be? His mouth is set in a tight grimace next.

Selwynn finally hands him a draft. Roland downs it quickly and looks at the empty glass with forlornness as if he's a regular alcoholic. I feel even more sorry for him then. I know now he wouldn't agree with any long-term plan Selwynn might have. Or what the others might come up with for social mixing; I guess he'll feel like this as long as his bitterness continues. I know, too, that if Roland continues to feel sorry for himself it'd be bad for him. In a way I want him to laugh, to be like his former self - especially when he clapped dominoes with the rest of us.

"It's not the end of the word, Roland," I say to him.

But Roland ignores me, he doesn't want my advice. And he's still talking about Suzan running off on him, saying it with more venom each time. Then he walks out of the bar, more dejected than ever.

Selwynn rubs his face; I guess now he isn't thinking seriously of his plan anymore. Maybe he's only thinking about Roland's sad state, just as I.

Selwynn says, "Maybe I too should have warned Roland about her."

"You knew her?" I ask quickly.

Selwynn doesn't answer my question. Then: "It would've have been of no use."

I look at him, wondering about this plan once more, while he mumbles to himself that perhaps Roland and the chick just happen to be different; ah, it was really a personal thing as Roland himself said - even though I begin to feel Roland meant more; how much more it was hard to tell.

Selwynn mutters loudly, "I guess Roland will become a woman-hater now."

"What about racial harmony?" I quickly say.

Selwynn's in no mood to answer this, even though he says, "I guess we just can't give up easily. We just can't, man! After all, we're here to stay!"

I nod and walk away from Selwynn's Bar, not sure what to think about. I guess, though, more than anything else I know that this isn't the end of Roland. Then I see him a week later. Behold! This time he's with another chick. Roland sees me now. Immediately he holds on to her very tightly as if this brunette is for keeps. He's smiling, too - once more with gladness in his heart.

I look at her carefully; she seems the bookish type with glasses and all. She appraises me as I walk up closer and greet Roland with a handshake. She's still looking at me with intelligent eyes, and smiling. Right away I begin thinking of Selwynn's plans of racial harmony.

"How do you do?" I mutter to her.

She smiles warmly; I smile also.

Roland grins a little sheepishly, looking unlike when he was with the blonde. Then he takes me aside, privately sort of. "Man, she's been after me a long time," he boasts and teases in the same breath: still with guile.

"But?" as I sense hesitation.

A little nervously now, Roland continues, "I won't let her leave me, man. I mean it! Wait an' see. Ask Selwynn, too -"

"Selwynn?"

"Yea, man. It's a plan alright. It's this harmony thing - she's all for it! She's a socio-"

"You mean that?"

"Yes. That what Selwynn says. What's the difference anyway?" he shrugs. "A chick's a chick." I figure Roland is still thinking of his former girlfriend. But just then she turns and looks at him, and Roland's colour fades immediately.

Again I'm thinking of Selwynn; maybe he has a hand in this. But as I look at Roland more keenly, I sense a new purpose in him cause his eyes begin to gleam like a man who's just received salvation. And she's still looking and smiling at me with ease sort of - as if she's beginning to have a strange power over me as well.

I nod to her. Suddenly she seems to understand what's going through my mind. But Roland immediately takes her by the hand and starts walking off. Alone, I start wonderin' about harmony in a different way than before. Without realizin' it I begin walking back to Selwynn's Bar to drink myself a couple of rounds - and to keep thinking about real harmony!

# THE RINK

George sits there, thinking of skating down the rink with the ease of a Guy LaFleur; he, a black man doing this thing with ease, though the more he thinks about it, the more it begins to boggle his mind. He's thinking too, that he, an islander, who has come to this country to establish roots, must really learn to skate: this same skating that looks so easy because he'll stand by the boards right here and watch people, especially the young ones, floating down the ice in the hockey rink as if they had skates on their feet from the day they were born. And such an amazing thing it is. More than ever he feels ashamed of himself not being able to skate...And how can a grown man living in Canada have difficulty doing such a simple thing, eh?

George is determined more than ever now, as he imagines going down the ice once more, doing twists and turns. A wide smile of anticipation sweeps across his face, his eyes brightening because he sees hismelf among these same kids, all of them, doing fantastic twists and turns. But it seems more difficult to do than he imagines, for just as he's about to make another attempt to shove off from the ice, nervousness overtakes him; he's more uncomfortable by the second the longer he remains looking around, with the skates on; and his heels now start to ache, his ankles burning. Yet, determined he is, and he struggles to get up, but slips down again. Pulling himself up once more, he still imagines going down the ice with twists and turns. He steps out a few feet now, away from the boards, and he sees himself going closer to the other end of the rink. He heaves, sucking in air, like someone taking his last breath, crimsoning as well. God, this skating is one helluva thing to do, he says to himself, gritting his teeth and swearing once more under his breath.

He's really taking his time now, trying his damndest not to fall again. He recalls falling down twice yesterday, once hitting his head heavily and nearly knocking himself out. Ah, this time it won't happen: he's taking greater care, being gingerly, more determined than ever; stepping out, one leg at a time stretching out like a strange tentacle or feeler. And it starts to feel good, slippery though it still is; yet he is moving, slightly, awkwardly nevertheless, going somewhere, and maybe all eyes are on him; yet he is fighting this feeling of self-consciousness creeping up inside him, black as he is. He grits his teeth harder.

At the same time he's thinking too of Boysie coming to visit him at one o'clock in the morning; Boysie should be ashamed of himself, knocking at his door at that ungodly hour, thinking he's still back on the island. And to think of it too, he didn't even phone before hand. Sure, lots of islanders and those from Guyana often do this, behaving without responsibility: as if they have no *civilization* in them. George moans, as he steps out farther, becoming more confident; indeed, skating is an easy thing after all, once you get the knack of it. Ha, he smiles a little. And he looks ahead, at the half a dozen or so kids by the sideboards who're looking at him, studying his every move. Aren't they? Watching him, they all are. Aren't they? Christ. And for a moment he imagines being one of them, being born and bred right here in Canada, in this cold, cold place. Does the cold really bother them as much as it does he now? George isn't reallly sure; as he takes another tentative step forward. Yes, he's out to show them, to show the world that he too can master this skill. He *will be* a Canadian after all. But the skates are starting to feel really heavy, as if his feet are cast in iron. Again he looks at the kids, sideways, their smiling faces: and one is pointing to him. But maybe they're really encouraging him, he thinks, and he must make another move, though his ankles are really burning like hell now. Oh God!

Yet another move forward: and the kids are watching him with increasing interest. For a second only, the skates start to feel different, almost like something fanciful, just as he'd once imagined. Another step forward, bolder as he is, gritting his teeth more than ever. As if encouraged, the kids come closer to the boards, leaning across: they're now almost in his line of vision, these same apple-cheeked, fluffy-headed-and-handsome kids, all smiling and making him really self-conscious. Suddenly George dares not move. He's even afraid to look at them; something is about to happen, something he fears; it's as if his legs are moving apart of their own accord, diagonally sort of, his heart beating faster, racing. And one of the kids bursts out laughing, nearly upsetting him fully this time. A flood of embarrassment rushes though him, in a wave; he's only five feet from the opposite side of the boards, and he knows he must make it, no matter what. He stretches his feet, pulling, trying to be mobile, though his ankles, heels, are really burning. Stretching out both hands next, he tries to lean forward too, to hold on to something for support. And again he looks at the kids, their eyes gleaming, these same ones who're smiling fully (even as he tries smiling himself to mask his shame). Ah, no one's going to stop him now. He will make it. Not even Boysie, coming at two o' clock in the morning; or Ida, his wife (pregnant as she is): the same Ida who's been laughing at him, telling him that he--an islander--will never be able to skate, since he wasn't born with ice in his veins! George winces. "Wha' d'you mean, woman?" he'd shot back at her, angry as hell; but Ida only laughed, her typical loud island-laughter, which echoed all around her, then added, "George, you're different, see. We--are. We've come from a hot-hot climate, and we weren't born with ice in our veins as I done tell you before." George replied almost immediately, anger burning in him, "But we...I..I want to be a--"He stopped and looked at her accusingly, questioningly, then blurted out, well...the rest of what he wanted to say: "That's why I came here!" He felt a little foolish saying this, incoherent as he'd become: Ida had a way of making him feel this way. He knew she was no longer listening to him. Maybe Ida was satisfied with the way things are, still wanting to remain an islander in Canada without ever changing. But why else did one come here?

The kids are laughing again, and three or four are leaning forward, over the boards, really close to him: as if they're watching a show in which--he, George Stanislaus Myers--is on centre stage. Seconds pass by. Then George, as if by a miracle, recovers his grip, holding on to the boards once again, on the opposite side (at last): and he remains standing there, proud, thinking he doesn't want to be like the other black immigrants in Canada. He wants to integrate, fully: and before long he'll be skating like the best of the native born-and-bred Canadians. He smiles, then at once stretches out his right leg, again, willing himself to go out, still thinking...what's the point of living in a new country if you have no intention of conforming to its ways, even though they are foreign ways! He wishes Ida would understand that sometimes...And just then, the unexpected happens--he falls...*braddacks*!

Like an enraged eel, George scurries and wriggles: and next he is spinning like a top, as he tries to get up, though his hands and legs are sprawled out, fully splayed; but again he's making every effort to really get up, difficult as it is, hoping that none of the kids see him. But it's too late, he knows: he can hear their loud laughter; and George sincerely hopes that they're not laughing at him; yet he tries not to look at them. As he twists and scrapes sideways, his heels aching (though he doesn't feel the pain as fully as before); and he gets up, then goes down again; then up once more, pushing, scrambling all the while. *But once more he goes down*!

The kids' shrill laughter rings in the air. And it's as if Ida and Boysie are also laughing with them, all together; the whole damn Caribbean island laughing! George is not sure what to do now. Sheer frustration grips him, and it's as if he's atrophied sitting there. Then, slowly, he turns, looking at the kids smiling; as much as he grins from ear to ear to hide his increasing discomfort. And more kids appear, some pointing to him for the benefit of others who are entering the arena.

George, play-acting now in a way, continues to grin, even though deep down he wishes he wasn't in this predicament. The kids are along the sideboards, and maybe they're beginning to think he's some sort of performer indeed, acting solely for their benefit. He reddens at once. And the kids draw much closer, some actually leaning over the boards, looking down at him, and one says, "Get up, Mister." Another adds a voice of encouragement, "Start, once more."

But George merely sits on the ice, as if that's all he can do now; yet he keeps grinning his grin of embarrassment, and he wishes he's never put on the blasted skates, gritting his teeth again as silent anger rises in him. Next he feels the cold deep under his pants; and he looks directly at these same apple-cheeked faces in his anguish and suddenly realizes that the kids are really offering him sympathy and encouragement: as if telling him that it's no shameful thing for a man who's learning to skate to be sitting flat on the ice the way he's doing now. And once more George tries pulling himself up; as the kids cluster about him, still offering encouragement. And he feels more of the cold seeping up under him: and suddenly he's thinking that this place isn't a cricket field he's sitting on, but sheer ice! Yet he's immobile, in a sort of daze...even as he next imagines Boysie looking at him, and laughing again: that same old island-laughter; Boysie telling him loud and clear, "What a damn fool you are, man. You's learnin' to skate, eh? What for? You know full well this ain't your kinda sport, George. Why you don't play cricket instead, man?" Boysie's laughter echoes all over, in the deepest areas of his mind, whirring in every cell in his brain; and Ida is also laughing–she and Boysie together, as if they'd planned it all along. George grimaces, and again tries pulling himself up, making a greater effort, yet he remains right there, looking at the kids: they in their winter clothes, their heavy gloves and red-and-blue toques. And no doubt they're wondering why he doesn't simply get up, because it's such an easy thing to do. Yes, George, it is. *Get up, man*!

Their combined laughter everywhere, as George surveys the innocent-as-babes' faces, suddenly wondering if they've ever seen a black man such as he (fully grown as he is) learning to skate, who's now flat on his backside; oh, what a ridiculous picture it must be!

Immediately, he wants to shout to them, to tell them to leave him alone. Yes, they must; but, instead, he merely sits there, knowing that if he tries again, he will fall once more. But George also knows that he can't sit there forever, with more kids coming in (some adults as well): and they're pointing at him, and laughing, sneering maybe. On a wild impulse, he heaves hard and tries getting up again...but he's really unable to budge. "What's the matter?" Boysie's voice in his head, again; adding: "Man, this aint a cricket field; this isn't like standing up straight-straight and hitting the ball *on de off side* across the green like Garfield Sobers or Clive Lloyd an' watching it shooting down to the boundary for four!"

At once George wants to tell the kids that, all twelve or thirteen of them, that he, sitting-down George, used to be one of the best batsmen on the island, and how the crowd used to cheer him loudly, like thunder ringing in his ears; oh, the sweet-sweet applause, that wonderful sound. Smiling, he watches them and keeps on reminiscing. Another boundary shot, four again...oh, the wild-wild applause! Right then one of the kids comes up and starts pulling his arm, assisting him to get up. Then another, three or four of them at the same time, urging him up. In no time, there's a dozen of them surrounding him, all these handsome faces; and George, realizing he needs their help, heaves, thankful for their assistance. In a final struggle, with skates and all, he pulls himself up. *Aaah*! He puts his hand to the back of his head, where there's a bump, which he remembers is the result of falling down heavily the first week he'd begun to learn to skate. He thanks the kids for their help even though, looking away from them, he silently swears under his breath.

Once more the kids laugh, goodhumoured as they are, such is their satisfaction and amusement: as they look at him standing with legs splayed out, like a pregnant woman. But George doesn't mind: he's happy to be standing up at all; and he knows now that he's had enough for one day. But he will come again tomorrow, and he's telling all these kids this, and maybe they'll be here to assist him once more. Yes, so intent he is to learn to skate, no matter what. Despite the taunts from Boysie and Ida. Or the kids looking at him...George once more swears because of the realization of his ineptitude: swearing more than in those days when he used to dream about coming to Canada and having to wait four long years for his immigration papers to be processed. And every time he thinks of the mother he has left behind: to whom he'll regularly send letters, with a ten-dollar bill in the envelope, and imagining the excitement on her face when she opened his letter with the bill falling out and landing close to her feet, like manna from heaven. But he's now stopped sending money when he realized that his mother wasn't really getting any (some *orangutan* postman in the district was stealing his hard-earned cash!). He recalls too that only after marrying Ida that he's stopped writing letters to his mother, all because he discovered her snooping around in his trouser pockets and wanting to read his letters: in a way Ida was trying to censor everything he wrote. Was it because she didn't want him to have anything to do with the island again?

After much contemplating, lying awake at nights, George suddenly decided to chart his own course, Ida or not. He'll be a real Canadian (though it isn't perfectly clear in his mind what a real Canadian is): thinking nevertheless that when he returns to the island on vacation he'll be flashing hundred-dollar bills before his mother's rheumy eyes and telling her in his best-acquired Canadian accent that he isn't the same short-pants, barefooted son who used to walk about the alleyways with raw sugar cane jutting out of his mouth. No, sireee! And there'll be a real gleam in her eyes, as he'll be telling her about all the progress he's made. Yes, black as he is, he will do just that. And who says no islander can make progress. George is smiling widely, and he figures he will be wearing collar-and-tie from morning to night since he'll no longer be working with his hands doing constructing work in Toronto like a whole lot of Italian immigrants, many of whom can hardly speak a word of English (though they've been living in Canada nearly all their lives), but only with his God-given brains, as a man is meant to work in the first place. Lord, why does it take a black man so long to realize this?

Ida greets him at the door, a smirk on her face. "George, you're back early today?" she says. George looks carefully at the beautiful woman standing before him, his *wife*, who has been trying to put him off his plan of action (there's no doubt about it). Ah, he will tell her to wait and see, that before long he'll skate like the best of the same ones she's so fond of watching on TV (it's not just Bill Cosbie). He looks at the skates in his hands dangling like a bunch of steel lobsters he has caught by the sea (memory of the island never far from his mind); but he also immediately recalls sitting down on the ice with his bottom freezing...and at once he walks past her to put the skates away.

Ida follows him.

George, sensing her presence, is starting to become angry, though he knows he must control himself: mock and tease as she is ready to do. But maybe she's simply crotchety since she became pregnant, he thinks to himself. He bends down into the cupboard, putting the skates away (though he looks longingly at them for a while, as if, suddenly, they are like cricket pads; and he smiles)). But Ida's closeness now really irks him. Right then the skates start appearing like a pair of ridiculous boots which only a strange breed of people wear: people who want to punish themselves for nothing at all. Ida, still close to him, the smirk on her face (which he knows), and he's seething inside; yet he's trying to control himself. Yes, Ida is really pregnant, he mutters to himself, her stomach already protruding.

But Ida is once more asking him why he's home so early. The mocking tone, her voice's hard edge. And he's forcing himself to think of something else: yes, hitting the cricket ball hard, and the loud applause, all the fluffy-faced ones indeed applauding as they watch the ball going down to the boundary for four! So happy he suddenly is, and he turns, facing Ida, and smiles widely. But Ida's lips are tightly pursed, and she says to him: "Is it true, George? Are you really skating?" "Yes, woman," he wants to shout at her; instead, he only mutters, not loudly enough: and self-consciously too the sound comes out of his throat like a grunt; and he's not sure what he's real saying now.

But Ida is at it again, lambasting: "But George, you can't blasted well be able to skate! You, a black man trying to do a white thing. It isn't the sport fo' you."

George angrily faces her; yet,again, he knows he must keep his cool, because only uncivilized people does lose their temper: these same ones who shout and swear like mad people even. And he's saying to her with his cold civilized eyes, *Leave me alone, woman. Leave me alone to do my thing in my own blasted way. Leave me, Ida, I done tell you!*

But Ida right then starts laughing in his face, telling him again that he'll never be good enough, no matter what. And George is no longer able to stand the irony in her voice. She's saying this thing loudly now: "You's one helluva black man, who's never gonna be different in this country! You hear me, George!" And, looking at her, he sees real pain in her eyes. For a while, as if not knowing what to do, how else to react, he smiles, an odd sort of smile, and maybe it's because he also knows that there's nothing else a man can do against the onslaught of a woman's tongue (especially a woman born-an'-bred on the island). He looks a little sheepishly at her, studying her serious face, like some sort of pity and terror written all over it, confusing him; gosh, he's never seen his woman looking like this before; yes, the same beautiful one he'd married: Ida now looking so damned serious–and ugly too.

***

Throughout supper, George is wondering about Ida's words: if she's right about the things she'd said. What if he will never be taken seriously in this country, no matter how hard he tries; no matter if he takes evening courses all his life as he struggles to better himself: determined as he is to match the best people, those same ones he and Ida often meet in the offices and stores and everywhere else, who're all professionals of one sort or another, and who sometimes make him feel inferior. And he tries to focus his thoughts on the rink, again: as if this is the solution, or escape; and he imagines skating down the rink once more with ease and a joyful rhythm, from one end to another. Ida watches him, as he slowly puts food into his mouth, chewing; and now he's looking at her without saying a word; she's also not speaking.

In bed that night, in their prolonged silence, Ida turns and twists, as if unable to bear the silence any longer. And George is also awake, thinking hard, about life's ways, about his own dreams and aspirations; and, vaguely, about the island, that village, the faces, his mother again, corrugated forehead, eyes wrinkled, pain. Ida in tears, her words, breaking the unbearable silence: "What's going through you' mind, George?" "Nothing," he lies. She turns again, once more to her side, still unable to sleep, this same soon-to-be heavy-bodied woman bearing his child. A three-month thing already, George is thinking, turning round right then and patting her stomach, putting an arm out to caress her: as if to touch the living thing he planted there in her, like some sort of miracle. Then, after a while, he recalls Boysie's face: Boysie still laughing, and saying: "Man-George, your first-born' gonna be a genius, gonna be my God-child too. Ha, ha."

George laughed then as well, amidst their drinking rum-and-coke: which was only a month ago. But now–suddenly– George makes up his mind that no *islander* is going to be the God-father of his child! He wants someone responsible, a native born Canadian (and it does not matter if this someone is white).

Ida twists and turns again, heavily, and asks, "Are you...well, thinking about our child, George?"

He doesn't answer. He only becomes more aware of her burgeoning roundness, in the darkness, the night's own reality, it feels like; and then the absolute smoothness of her flesh under a pink nightgown (the same one he'd bought for her on her last birthday). He rests his hand against her wide-awake heart (as he tells himself), now beating rapidly: so rapidly that he can almost hear it. And he thinks right then of a daughter being born: a child with a stout heart no less, this same one who will make him (and Ida too) very proud. And he imagines taking her to learn to skate, in that same rink; and he's convinced this child will learn quickly, such will be her determination. He smiles; but the smile quickly fades when he remembers falling down earlier that day, and the kids around him, laughing, pulling his arms up: "Get up, Mister. Yes,you must!"

Like a film unwinding before his mind's eye, the kids once more all about him, urging him up: and George is anxious not to remain much longer on the cold ground. "Get up, it's easy to do, Mister," he hears, and this time it's the voice of his own child: black as she is, yet apple-cheeked (how amazing); she's urging him more than all the others, *to get up, now*! As he sits there, bewildered. Right then, he is looking around, and he sees a large crowd of people (mostly adults), all looking at him: at them! Who're ready to applaud. George at once pulls himself up with the assistance of this same black child, and stands there with a new-found pride. Turning, he looks at the crowd and, then, bows. Next, he looks at the middle of the rink: as if he's compelled to; and there he sees her, his daughter, with skates on, all alone: she, the star, doing this miraculous thing indeed–skating, pirouetting, as if she was born with skates on; her doing more twists and turns, and leaps as well, and smiling all the while, dazzling almost.

A further round of applause. And George stands by the boards, and also applauds, marvelling at this child he and Ida have brought into this world: who's skating with such ease and grace. "George, you okay?" he hears. But he has started chuckling, not wanting to stop this good feeling inside him, which is welling up like a tide; and he's not sure if he's still dreaming or is fully awake.

"George, you sure you's okay?" Ida's voice: she, turning once more, to his side. "Remember, Boysie coming to see us again soon. Man, you should take he to learn to skate. The two o' you islanders!" She smiles in the darkness, still in her half-asleep state. And yet she continues muttering, "This skating, George, maybe you're determined, are you not?" It's as if she's not waiting for an answer, turning fully and looking at his wide-awake eyes, and how he's still chuckling.

But George is also thinking hard, and is throwing his arms about her, and saying close to her ears: "Yes, Ida, I'm going to take Boysie to learn how to skate: he, the God-father, no? Yes, I will; it's something he's bound to know how to do. Ha, ha; and this child inside o' you, she'll skate better than both of us. Ha, ha." He keeps repeating this, as Ida frowns: not sure what's going through his mind. But George seems unable to suppress the gladness overtaking him: and the grace and ease with which his child is still pirouetting, and all the world is watching, applauding her...as Ida presses closer, looking fully at him in the dark, with her wide-awake eyes brimful with tears of her own sweet joy.

# ALL THE KING'S MEN

Starkie Peterson Mulligan (or simply SP, which sometimes stands for "Sugar Plantation," because of his habit of always walking around with a joint of sugar-cane jutting out of his mouth and jauntily swinging his arms about): he scoffed at the air itself, his forehead like a pillar to the sky. Then suddenly his mouth opened, like a trap door (some said), eyes swirling. Yes, Starkie–the one and only. And I am thinking of him still back there on the island dreaming of one day coming to Canada like the rest of us. Fellas are clapping cards and playing dominoes in the Jane-Finch area in Toronto and now and again recalling Starkie...and laughing harder. And let them now hear what I have to say, as I am on the phone to my pal Harro (short for Harris). "You hear the news, man?" I say.

"What news?"

"Starkie, our own Sugar Plantation–Starkie Peterson Mulligan–you forget him?"

Harro starts laughing, and is reminiscing at once. "No one forgets that dude back there," he says.

"You have it wrong, Harro."

"Wrong?"

"Starkie's right here–in Canada!"

Harro is taking his time to allow this to sink in; then he laughs in a giddy sort of way, his entire face in a tremor, nerve-ends twitching, I can tell.

"It's true," I emphasize.

Harro is laughing now, saying this can't be true. "Not S.P. Mulligan, a poorarse man like he! He can't be here!" Harro is serious now, his face grim, it's not hard to tell.

But I am thinking how life can turn out different for some of us in this same cold country; and, maybe, for a man like Starkie things can also dramatically change. Yet I say to Harro, apologetically almost: "That's what I been hearing, man–he's here–right here wid us!"

"When he come, eh?" Harro is getting round to accepting what all along appears incredible.

"Seems like, well...a few years ago."

"A few years?"

I figure Harro's eyes are now bulging out in surprise–the Jamaican that he is...but what does it matter what island...we're all the same here, though there are some who're *Anglo-Blacksons*, trying to outdo white people in their quiet, reserved ways.

"He been living right here in Toronto, see," I add. "An' hiding too all this time, it seems; though he's also been attending university."

"University?" Harro is aghast.

It's the God's truth, I tell him.

I expect him to burst out laughing once more, a real loud peal–cause this university business is really confusing him, more than I think it would. "York University, where else?" I add. I guess I am ready to ridicule Starkie and the university all at once; and I am also laughing right then 'cause I know Harro has been taking courses at George Brown Community College for as long as I know, trying to get a diploma in Business Administration...for the past seven years! Whereas Starkie, who has come here–illegally no doubt–is now a *qualified* dude: the same one we used to call "Sugar Plantation!"

Harro grunts at the other end like a man with a sudden sickness; but once more he's laughing *kya-kya-kya*, and maybe his tongue is stretching out like a lizard, and panting next from this sudden exertion.

Harro, of course, is not used to such displays of emotion: though now it's different–all on account of Starkie. I also start laughing, like nervous reaction. Harro adds, "Man, this is a miraculous thing–for one of we very own Caribbean people, I mean." He laughs again, then stutters: and I'm not sure what is really going through his mind. But suddenly he sounds nervous and anxious, as he adds, like a reminder:

"That Starkie's one of we, man. We should be proud of him."

I agree, but I am also thinking (as much as Harro no doubt) of the past: when Starkie'd walk around aimlessly in the district; and how at school, old Headmaster Morgan would let fly a dozen lashes on his backside until sparks flew out. God, then Starkie would holler as if he was about to be murdered! Once he'd bolted out of the school, and Mr

Morgan sent us chasing after him. But Starkie really ran fast then, outsprinting ther best of us! And some of us thought madness had overtaken him. D'you remember that, Harro? I now ask.

Harro murmurs more of the details on the phone, though I fill in the gaps of that memorable episode. He adds, "Yes–we chased after him; we really did! But Starkie was too fast; and yeah, later we searched everywhere fo' he, all through the canefields. Through blacksage and carrion-crow bush we searchin', an' still there was no sign of he. We figured he'd be sleeping in the graveyard that night. An' maybe, yes–Starkie been dead. Dead, I say!" Harro pauses, catching his breath.

"That was what Starke tol' us a week later when he finally came back to the school," he adds. "How he made friends with the dead...and from then on, no one could harm he, not even Headmaster Morgan! We believed him; we really did!"

"Yes, Harro. Even Mr Morgan believed him, cause he made a long speech to the full gathering of us. Remember how he made us stand up–until our heels ached! And he kept telling us 'bout good behaviour without once mentioning Starkie's name. But we all knew he was referring to Starkie...as if Starkie was suddenly the paragon of virtue.

"And right after that, Starkie started telling us the truth–that he survived 'cause the Devil himself brought food everyday to the tombstone where he'd been sleeping...for that entire week! You remember Harro? Starkie an' the Devil, the two o' them alone, talking all night long on the tombstone!

"Yes, and Starkie's grandmother, old and crochety as she was, Grandma Doherty," I muttter on, everything vivid in my mind's eye, "she started coming to the school and talking to Mr Morgan, as if they were old pals."

Harro adds, "And Starkie kept boasting 'bout knowing the Devil, an' how his Grandma taught him many things which no else knew about." Harro is remembering more of the details, surprising me in a way.

"Yeah, Harro, Starkie started showing off his money too, dollar bills, causing us to open our eyes wide-wide. An' then he started passing around sweets too, like manna from heaven, and laughing like a man really gone mad."

"He put the fear in we, and to think all along Starkie been getting the money and the sweets from the fella goin' out with his unmarried mother, Stella–in another part of town. Yes, that same buxom and stylish woman, she and that red-skinned nigger-man who they say was rich-rich, who owned a sweet factory, and he been giving money to Starkie all along–all the dollar notes!"

Harro moans, then once more reminds me how really dunce Starkie was.

"See, that ole woman, his Grandma Doherty, maybe she did something to he then, 'cause she kept coming to see Mr Morgan, maybe to make him do something–rheumy-eyed and hair white-white like chalk as she was; and, her eyes like holes on a cardboard wall in a ramshackle house. Maybe she cast a spell on Mr Morgan–'cause he never wanted to thrash again. Never!"

"I know."

Then Harro pauses, coughing a little, before muttering: "He's one of we, though. Maybe we should be proud of he, that Starkie Mulligan-Sugar Plantation and all."

Again he pauses, thinking; then he adds: "But we can't call him that anymore."

Maybe Harro's now imagining the island, that sunshiny place, all those "faery isles" where we came from. But I also expect him to burst out laughing; however, he simply says: "That man can go on to greater things, see."

He chuckles next, which has me wondering what thoughts are really going through his mind. Then Harro starts talking about the progress of the black race, as if we're God's chosen people, the way some others boast (like the Jewish people for instance: all their achievements in intellect and science and politics, things sometimes too difficult for me to understand). But Harro keeps on talking, as if living in this snow-bound land has really addled his mind. Or, is it Starkie's achievement (or magic) that now has him so truly confused that he's talking about things that are, well...beyond him. Or, maybe, it's his wife Inez, who's something else, I tell you.

He adds, "We can't let this pass by, man. We can't!"

"What you mean, Harro?"

I can tell Harro's thinking real hard, the sheer memory of Starkie now overwhelming him. And yet he is reminiscing: "Oh, that Starkie. He used to cant his eyes like a crazy dude when walking down the street, but all the time it's the intelligence in those same eyes, man."

I imagine Harro's own eyes swirling; next he's recalling other things about Starkie–more clearly than ever: a whole bunch of little things, all vividly, and really amazing me.

I am a little nervous now though; then I remind Harro that Starkie used to be the biggest dunce in the district, maybe in the entire island. We couldn't all have been wrong.

But I sense Harro shaking his head, and now in a very solemn way, he says:

"That Starkie's one of we own. He represents us in this white-white snow-laden land, Bachelor of Arts as he is. I'm really proud of him, and so should you, Monty."

I am awed by Harro's manner, strange as it is.

Harro lets out next, like a strange incantation: "Bachelor of Arts....Bachelor of Arts."

I am becoming frightened now, the more I listen to him muttering, like a sickness as he adds, "I'm proud of him. I am!"

"Proud?" I ask.

"Yes, man–he's better than we."

It's really a new side to Harro, which I've been observing of late maybe; all on account of Inez: her influence on him–cause she'd been attending seminars about human rights and social development and spewing out all sorts of new-fangled ideas about black people having to appreciate their dignity and self-esteem cause we're in a new country--Canada–and about all sorts of other minority people (Chinese and East Indians and Natives) being *marginalized* all these years–and it's time things change; some of which must be rubbing off on Harro, I'm convinced.

Harro adds: "In Starkie we're seeing a living example of human development, how our people who've had barriers placed on them yet can achieve greatness."

"Greatness?"

"Our Starkie Peterson Mulligan, Bachelor of Arts, man; he has climbed to great heights!"

I'm not sure about Harro any longer, even as I mull over his words, trying not to start laughing.

"He's better than us," adds Harro.

"Is he?" I ask, incredulous.

"It's a heroic feat, man."

"Heroic, eh?" I instinctively recall Starkie walking around with that idiotic grin on his face.

But Harro starts explaining how he knew all along that Starkie would climb to great heights, especially after his inventing such a story about sleeping in the graveyard and being close to the Devil, and then outwitting Mr Morgan, which no one had ever done before. Surely Starkie must be a genius; and now is the time for the greatness to flourish.

"He will rise high, that Starkie," proclaims Harro. "An' we must acknowledge him, black as he is. We must celebrate his achievement!"

"Celebrate?" I say softly, figuring now that something's truly the matter with Harro. And I am also thinking of Inez and what whe must have been saying round the house, all those new ideas now swirling in

Harro's head. But Harro chuckles hard, I swear to it. I wish right then I could see his face, just as I am eager to see Starkie's, and perhaps–to *celebrate*!

It's a party the like we've never had in a long time. "San Fernando" Singh, "Cod Liver Oil" Beharry, "Bajan" Ho Sang (whose cousin was the best jockey in Barbados), "Big Eye" Blaine, "Congo" Wharton, and "Lingua Franca" Stephens–who still insists that all languages derive from Swahili (because "Africa is the cradle of civilization")–and a host of other fellas, some high class and others low class and underclass, are all here. And many too are from *mixed-up* classes sporting the latest fashion with their best threads on and showing off the best new-wave hairstyles–on this occasion of celebration for our famous brother, Starkie Peterson Mulligan, Bachelor of Arts!

Harro and I have done a great deal of organizing for this special event. Now though I am a little surprised when Harro, smiling (as if he knows something I don't), says that he–with Inez's help–will be the "Entertainment Director," especially since he's met with a couple of rasta-cum-reggae cats who only want free booze and will play at the party for nothing.

"It would be jus' like back home," Harro says, almost laughing.

I look at Inez, smiling; and I am beginning to become suspicious. I also remember Inez's words to Harro about human social development, and how the black race shouldn't miss out on it. I say, "You sure Starkie's goin' to like all this? I mean, we haven't see him in years? What if he has changed?"

"Impossible," Harro replies, clapping me on the shoulder. "A man like Starkie can never really change, Bachelor of Arts an' all. Just wait an' see"; and Inez adds, "An islander is an islander, no matter where he is. Be cool, Monty." And Harro looks at his wife and nods, which has me even more puzzled.

I continue to have my anxieties, especially after finally contacting Starkie on the phone–to hear him speak in an affected manner: a very proper Queen's English, accent and all, as if he's just come from Oxbridge itself.

But Harro's enthusiasm keeps me buoyed up, and I figure that if Starkie doesn't show up, Harro will turn things around; he will say it's really a special party, well...for his wife Inez, who's all smiles. I turn from her to the other guests arriving, many not too sure what the party's all about.

Then Inez says to me, "Where's Starkie? He shoulda be here by now. It getting late. It's after nine now."

"He is coming," I say, though I am not sure any longer.

"I will make a special mix for him, you wait and see," she says, noting the worried look on my face; and just then she smiles in a teasing manner, and marches off to the kitchen, while I concentrate on her tight-fitting dress, the way it hugs her hips and she's looking like a really desirable island-woman. Then I turn to see Harro greeting some others, their long arms dangling at their sides; only Ho Sang has decided to bring a bottle of booze, classy champagne–I can tell; and maybe he already knows all about Starkie's recent achievement.

Harro is still smiling all the while: not anxious, like me; especially when half an hour goes by and still there's no sign of Starkie. Then Harro, now looking somewhat troubled, says, "You sure Starkie coming, man?" "Yeah," I reply. "You did phone him to tell him we're having a party to honour someone special, no?"

Again I nod, recalling Starkie's promise to come–in perfect Queen's English (though reluctant too he sounded, as I recall).

"Where in the hell is that man, though?" Harro cries out.

"You think the Devil gone wid him?" Ho Sang asks, bursting out with a laugh.

A few fellas turn around and look at him.

So does Inez, coming in from the kitchen, a fresh dab of lipstick accentuating her attractive face.

Harro turns from her to me, once more: "That man's really playing de fool, Devil or not."

"He just might have changed, Harro," I add, apprehensive, turning to look at the others; and I notice "Big Eye" Blaine making a move to get the attention of fair and willowy Bernice, the sister from Panama; while "Congo" Wharton is eyeing Eunice "the Beautiful" Blair, even as he begins crooning by himself; which causes "Cod Liver Oil" to laugh loudly and pretend to be gay–because Toronto is a city full of gays.

A loud burst of laughter follows.

For a while everyone forgets the guest of honour, though my eyes are peeled to the door. I also notice Inez going off to the corner to stir the punch, as if preparing a witch's brew. Then looking at me she grins, tempting me to go up to her...and maybe to ask her what's cooking. But just then "San Fernando" Singh rolls his eyes at her like a dreamer; and he starts patting me heavily on the shoulder, a sign that he's already been drinking too much.

I look at Inez again, but "San Fernando" holds me by the collar, insisting, "If our guest of honour don't come, man, we're still goin' to have a good time. Yeah, Inez, married as she is, is one special gal."

"So she is, San Fernando–so she is."

Other fellas now start fidgeting. But Harro, a little nervous (I can tell), at once pulls a chair under him, and steps onto it as if on a pulpit. He begins: "Ladies an' gentlemen, I wish to draw to your attention..." he coughs a little, clearing his throat like a seasoned speaker given to long and spellbinding oratory, even as he's thinking about what he should say next.

"As I've been saying about our honoured guest, Starkie Peterson Mulligan, whom you all remember, but have not set eyes on for a long time now: I want to reassure you he will be here at any moment."

Again Harro coughs, still nervous and solemn, though making light of the matter. And fellas, especially "Lingua Franca," cry out, "Yeah, man, where is he?" Others at once clap their hands. Harro adds: "Indeed, it will be a shameful t'ing if Starkie don't show up at all; I mean, my goodlookin' woman Inez and I have done a lot of preparing for this important occasion; all on account o' Starkie, who's here in Canada, and this same party's in his bestowed honour!"

(APPLAUSE)

"It won't be the end of the world," continues Harro, "cause we West Indians know how to have a good time, guest or no guest."

"Yeah-yeah," a few others chorus at once.

Harro laughs, and waves to me, and I wave back automatically.

Other fellas continue laughing; though a few–I can tell–really wish to see Starkie now.

Harro's sing-song island accent once more: "We people does enjoy weself good, you see–especially when we have the best free music, an' the best free food an' the best–" again he stops, for dramatic effect, and he clears his throat; which causes laughter once more. "Yes, as I been saying, the best blasted women in this city too–we have right here! Heh-heh-heh!"

"Hear-hear," comes another chorus–especially from Inez, and Eunice, and her sister Bernice, all applauding loudest.

Harro is now waxing into form, the charmer that he is; and once he's in the mood, he's hard to stop, I figure, turning to look at the door once more. Good old Harro, I say to myself, he should've been the one to celebrate getting a Bachelor of Arts degree. Hasn't he been dreaming about this for years? I look at Inez again, who is smiling and thinking the same as I do no doubt.

Winkie, the Steelband and Reggae Stud-Ace, is now really laughing, though he's itching to show off his talents at the guitar once more, the crooner too that he is.

But it is Harro who is waving his hands about and still declaiming, as if he's forgotten all about Starkie.

Suddenly who should walk in–but Starkie Peterson Mulligan, in tuxedo and top hat and looking really distinguished, which causes Harro's eyes to nearly fall out of their sockets. And mine too, for that matter, so surprised I am. Other fellas are also awestruck, their mouths hanging open, especially since they see leaning on both sides of Starkie's arms are two tall, attractive blondes who're smiling widely, in complete contrast to the solemn, but dignified look (so it seems) on Starkie's face.

Harro stops talking as if he's hit by a bolt of lightning.

The music also stops.

The blondes titter, unabashed as they seem. I notice one with a dimple, and Starkie hugs her tightly, as if he figures at once what's going through my mind.

But it is Starkie I am really looking at, at how much taller he is; how dashing too. No wonder he has these two lovely ladies by his side, leaning against him as if he's the Rock of Gibraltar. Yet, I figure it's the same old Starkie, dignified expression or not. And maybe Harro's thinking the same, even as he seems rivetted to silence.

I turn and look for Inez, but she's nowhere in sight.

Now Starkie has the floor, it seems: he, our honoured guest; and Harro must humour him, his pretension and all. And extending a hand to Starkie, he says, "Welcome, brother."

But Starkie is aloof, ignoring the hand; which leaves Harro grinning a little stupidly and muttering:

"Man, you know me, don't you? You rememba me, no?"

Other fellas also stretch out their hands, as if they are now eager to touch the honoured flesh.

But Starkie turns away with a flourish, and nods to the blondes--and at once leads them to where the drinks are, as if he knows this well in advance. And to where the food is (which I didn't know myself).

Inez now eyes him all the while, smiling: the only one really smiling.

"Cod Liver Oil" boldly walks up to Starkie, and not to be outdone says: "Man, aren't you the same fella, well, I mean, the same like the rest of we--you, Starkie "Sugar--?"

"Mr S.P. Mulligan, Bachelor of Arts--if you please," scolds Starkie, lifting his head high and almost glowering at the speaker before him.

"Okay-okay, man; you're an educated dude an' all," adds "Cod Liver Oil," slinking away.

Then it is "Lingua Franca's" turn as he says to Starkie: "Say, man, you've done well fo' yourself. But how's that grandmother o' yours back home? You bring she across, poorarse an' black as you is?"

Starkie immediately turns away from him in contempt, and faces

Ho Sang–who is suddenly diffident and nonplussed all in one.

Starkie lifts his head a little higher, and puts a piece of barbecued chicken into his mouth (which I now realize Inez had specially prepared for the occasion:and only Starkie, prescient as he is, knew about). From the way Starkie is enjoying the chicken, I figure Inez has prepared it with the best West Indian sauce.

Starkie looks at the blondes from the corners of his eyes, and then glares at me. And he keeps stripping the chicken into tiny parts, which he elegantly dangles over his nostrils. Then he relishes the smell of each part of stripped chicken, before licking his lips. Next he says to the blondes bracing against him:

"These are the kind of people I've been telling you about. How they'd look up to me; so I will be their leader, you understand. Now I am!"

"Leader?" cry out a few voices in surprise.

Starkie ignores them, stripping more of the chicken, which he dangles before his nostrils like a man about to perform a miracle.

"You see, girls," he says, "they're honouring me–the best among them; I, the same Sugar Plantation Mulligan, the same local boy-cum-folk hero. I now command their full respect and admiration, which is why they've decided to hold this party for me. I will champion their cause in this same temperate land against white people. I will be lobbying on their behalf since I have the confidence that none of them has to meet politicians of all stripes, from all parties, and businessmen, mayors and governors. I will be meeting them on their behalf, black and underpriveleged–as they all are!"

More strips of chicken disappear into his mouth, and he laughs hard, gloating in a fashion. He adds: "Yes, I have the right contacts–and all black men shall respect me!"

The blondes, as if in a new-found admiration of Starkie, giggle loudly. Then Starkie turns left, then right: as everyone else watches in further awe, wondering what next he will do or say.

Starkie lifts his head higher, more aloof than ever, as if this is a practiced act that none can emulate. And he swallows more of the stringy chicken: this very act which now begins to appear like a work of art.

In a corner, watching carefully, Inez smiles; she mutters something in Harro's ear. And I turn to Starkie once more; this time the image of his being thrashed by Headmaster Morgan and then being visited by the Devil enters my mind; and I want to burst out laughing. Yet I keep looking at him; how solemn and lordly he appears, strips of chicken and all.

And Inez is really smiling, unfaze as Starkie lifts his head higher and enunciates slowly: as I am thinking how education can really transform a man.

Harro, close to me now, whispers: "You think he gone mad?"

"I don't know, Harro."

Starkie, grandly, adds: "In this country, a man must know himself; he must look ahead, not sideways or backwards; but always ahead, to the better things in life. So I say a black man must also keep the right company if he will continue to lead the flock." He pauses, and when he speaks again, it is to say an even more suprising thing: that he has political ambition in this promised land of Canada!

I mutter to myself, "Starkie's really goin' beyond himself."

Harro eyes me in incredulity, and I figure that perhaps he really believes in all that Starkie is saying now, so convincing is the oratory.

Starkie continues for another fifteen minutes, each time the blondes chuckling in approval, like a well-rehearsed act. And other fellas are also chuckling, amazing as it is.

From the corner of my eyes I see Inez moving towards the bowl containing the punch. She is...well...putting some added ingredients into it; all the while as Starkie is enunciating with greater care–like a man who has just stepped through the doors of Oxbridge University and referring to all sorts of famous economists and historians and literary figures (as I think they are) all in the same breath.

I can't help asking myself, What is the matter with Starkie, showing off his learning like this?

Inez starts passing around the punch, her special libation it seems, making sure the bowl goes right under Starkie's nose.

Starkie sniffs, crinkling his nose and curling in his lips, then wiggles his ears: as if to accentuate his lordly manner (though one or two fellas later recall they'd seen him do this on the island). The blondes are also sniffing, and fellas start laughing.

When Starkie starts drinking the punch, like a thirsty peelnecked creole fowl, I am not too surprised. And Inez's eyes light up the more Starkie drinks; she keeps offering the bowl to him, and watches the glint in his eyes. Glass after glass, Starkie pours down his throat, as if punch is going out of style; which makes me think that even the best of us can act no different when some things are free. "Drink up, Starkie," encourages "San Fernando" Singh, carried away by the rhythm of Starkie's head-bobbing manner.

Starkie throws his head back, like a rooster–and swallows heavily.

The blondes applaud.

But Starkie is having his glass refilled by a smiling, solicitous Inez–for the seventh time. And again he swallows quickly, gulping it all down. I figure that Starkie's also trying to entertain the fellas, showing them how much he can really consume.

Applause follows–as he wipes his mouth; the blondes still applauding.

Then it dawns on me that it is the blondes who're really establishing the cue for us to applaud; this too being part of their act.

I look at Inez smiling, the bowl of punch in her hands, ready to offer it to Starkie once more.

I figure she's up to something.

I keep an eye on Harro as well–but it's hard to tell what he's really thinking, though he smiles from time to time (but Harro also has a worried look on his face). Other fellas jostle about Starkie, all eager to hear him speak.

Starkie gesticulates to all and sundry, his eyes starting to bulge unnaturally. Something's the matter with him now. Inez smiles again. But Starkie holds my attention, as he says:

"Man, education is the thing. Blacks are God's special people, you see. They're the last tribe. Start believing in the power of your minds and you shall bring about the change in this white country, which is also yours. The mind is all, I tell yuh, and it is no more streamin' an' technical education only for Black children in the schools here in Toronto and Halifax and in other cities across this snow-laden land. Gird thy loins, I say, and make sure your young ones reach the highest level in these same schools so far away from the Babylon of the Caribbean. Yes, let them emulate me!"

Immediately he looks at the blondes, and one cries, "Yes, let them emulate him!"

The fellas at once start tittering; a few also applauding, "San Fernando" Singh loudest.

Starkie adds: "See, fellas, we blacks have come from an advanced civilization. Yes, right there in Africa, in that ancient land, where some of the mightiest kings and queens, mightier than those even of Greece and Rome of classical times, I say." When he curls in his lips, it's as if he is suddenly transformed into Yoruba or Ashanti royalty, not unlike what I've seen in a calendar given out by the Nigerian Consulate.

Starkie adds, "The white race has been keeping our history from us, brothers and sisters. But I say it's time we begin learning for ourselves, to take pride in our own." He pulls in his chest, eyes swirling; and indeed he is the Yoruba king (I say to myself).

But then–suddenly–Starkie breaks into creolese:

"Yeah, fellas, de first docta was a black man, see; yeah, de first mathematician was a black man named Potlemy; an' de first warrior, de greatest o' dem all who tek de elephants across a mountain, was called Hannibal, which no white man's been able to do ever since! So what we need now is to have de white race cooperatin' wid us, to express mutual affection,the same as we been doin' for centuries!"

The blondes chirp, as Starkie adds:

"We black people can continue to improve the lot of mankind, if you elect me! ELECT ME!" He raises both hands in the air, and the blondes ring out, "Yes, elect him! ELECT HIM!"

Immediately the band starts up, as if this too has been well-planned in advance–by Starkie himself no doubt, amazing as it is. And "Big Eye" Blaine starts dancing with one of the blondes, while "Lingua Franca" sporting a goatee which seems to cover his sleeves each time he juts his head back and forth, then sideways like an agitated ramgoat, tries to outdo everyone else. The rhythms pound and throb; the air itself whirring.

Starkie sips more of the punch, and looks at the band in a dazed way. Winkie and his reggae partner are now trying to outdo themselves, celebrating *the man's return*!

When Starkie starts tapping his toes, everyone is doing the same. Next Starkie is dancing all by himself, eyes closed as he throws his arms into the air and hops about like an athlete trying to warm up before a big race. And fellas are doing this also, like a strange but ancient African dance known only to the Yoruba king. *Yes, emulate him*!

I turn to Harro, and with his eyes he's telling me, "But, that man wants to be Prime Minister of this temperate land, full as he is with tropical madness and devilry, eh." I move closer to Harro, and mutter:

"Starkie's gone mad. Look at he good, look how he lifting up his arms and throwing them about. Is only crazy people does do that, man."

Inez also comes closer, "It's the punch, you see," she says, looking at me, smiling.

"The punch?" I ask.

"Yes," and she turns away, tapping her toes too, for she also is enjoying herself. And now everyone is circling about Starkie, clapping their hands in accompaniment of Starkie's antics. Indeed, Starkie looks totally ridiculous now, like a sort of clown, his hands waving in the air all the time.

But the others are clapping their hands, tapping their toes, *for he is their leader*! Starkie's eyes gleaming in triumph, his face expanding like a gargoyle's; and more and more he waves his hands about to the beat of the rhythm–which "Big Eye" Blaine likes nothing better, for he too is enjoying the attention one of the blondes is giving him, embracing him as he gyrates–from waist down, limbo style.

Things now really start getting out of hand, and I figure it's time

I do something–for Starkie's one of us, Bachelor of Arts and all. This man shall not be an embarrassment to the Black race, I quietly say, nodding to Harro and saying to him: "Sugar Planation's one of we own, man. We better stop this gallivantin'."

But Harro looks sadly at me.

I determinedly move forward.

"Starkie, you are..." I begin, then stop.

But it is Harro who now lets out loudly, "You're drunk man. You're drunk, Starkie!"

"A little inebriated, that's all, brothers," Starkie hollers back, then explodes with laughter.

All the fellas are also laughing, including "Cod Lover Oil" Beharry the loudest.

Then Starkie turns to "Lingua Franca"– who still has one of the blondes leaning on him, so taken he is with her. Starkie nods, encouraging her to "accommodate one and all." Next Starkie smiles gleefully, his hands raised as he whirls about.

I figure at once it's the old evil spirit coming out in him, even as Starkie's voice rises above mine:

"I am your leader–behold!" Then he looks directly at me, adding: "I am, like the Lord on high." Starkie suddenly looks like a veritable high priest in an ancient religious ceremony, tall as he is, and repeats that he is our leader.

"Amen, amen," a few fellas chant, amazing as this too is.

Now I can't tell if the fellas truly believe in him or if they're simply play-acting. Harro also seems puzzled, I can tell. The other blonde is moving closer to Starkie again, waiting for the next cue no doubt.

But Starkie merely grins and embraces her in a wide sweep, then pulls the other blonde away from "Lingua Franca" so they're once more close to him. And loudly he cries out:

"Griselda and Gretchen, my true sisteren, behold the black sheep before me as they all are. I am the leader of this same flock which is astray in this temperate land. Yes, I am, preordained as it is. And you see how they're honouring me, one and all. Ha, ha!" Then Starkie's eyes swirl and cant, like a bull about to be beheaded; and again I glance at Harro, who looks really concerned now. He glances at Inez still enjoying every moment of it.

She nudges me and whispers, "Just wait an' see."

"Eh?" I ask.

"Wait an' see," she repeats, laughing.

Once more Starkie whirls, but just then falls flat on the floor; so exhausted he is...in a drunken stupor.

At once fellas are all around him, looking at Starkie's wide-opened eyes and muttering about the Devil being with him!

Harro says, "It's no mean thing; I mean, being Bachelor of Arts."

By now I'm thinking that indeed it's the Devil that's causing Starkie to behave like this; to perspire so much, even as he's still lying flat on the floor. This same Devil that he has brought with him to Canada, and which is now letting him down. And I am really alarmed now, wondering, What if he should die right here!

But Inez, as I figure she would, comes closer to me, nudging me and telling me to remain cool. And so does Harro, laughing, in contrast to the alarm all around.

It dawns on me right then that Harro and Inez planned this all along, to have Starkie lying flat on his back, this lordly and pretentious one. Yeah, have a really good look at him, fellas, Bachelor of Arts as he is an' all!

Harro mutters, "Blessed are some men who have knowledge, but unemployed as they are."

"Unemployed?" I ask.

Everyone looks at us: looking at Harro, waiting for him to say more; while the blondes continue wiping the perspiration from Starkie's face with tender loving care.

Harro nods. Inez also nods.

Harro adds,"And the greed of some men, falling prey to something as simple as West Indian punch. It never fails. This freeness never fails!" He winks at his wife, whose eyes light up at once.

But then, suddenly, it's as if we're all in it; from the beginning, aren't we?

And I am also looking down on him, thinking of a wastrel in a backwater island alleyway. And why this thought keeps going through my mind now, I don't really know; though I am also thinking of the Devil, shaking my head in disbelief–and wishing Starkie would get up right then and once more strut about in his affected Oxbridge manner.

Harro, close to me, whispers: "Great as we are, we must come to recognize our weakness first." He turns, looking at all the fellas, expecting them to say "Amen."

But everyone is silent.

A soft moan escapes Starkie's drunken lips, like a final affirmation of the absolute truth of Harro's words.

And Harro looks at Starkie once more, with a serious face, then at Inez; as if really wishing him to get up so he could truly be the leader of the black race; the one and only. Yes, *the one and only*!